CONTENTS

Chapter 1 – Introduction

I wrote the Freedom Programme in 1998 after working in Probation Service Perpetrator Programmes. Since then, I have heard hundreds of firsthand accounts from women who have escaped from abusive relationships because they have attended the Freedom Programme or read my books 'Living with the Dominator' and the 'Freedom Programme Home Study Course'. Others have escaped because they joined the Freedom Programme Forum which is an online community for women who need information and support to deal with abusive partners. The complete Freedom Programme is now available online in a variety of languages.

Women, girls, men and boys have now sent me their harrowing accounts stories of childhood abuse and violence. I have included them in this book. Women have chosen to be identified by the name of a flower.

I have also trained thousands of 'professionals' to facilitate the Freedom Programme and the majority of these trainees have also been survivors. They have also told me that, until they did my sessions on the 'Effects of Abuse on Children' in the programme, they had blamed themselves for failing to protect their children. After completing this session, many said they "finally realised" that the blame lies with the Dominator and not with them. When we do become aware of how our children have been affected by the Dominator, we often say "I wish I had left sooner" and we blame ourselves. However, the only acceptable and responsible reply is: *"You left when you could. If you could have left sooner you would have done so!"*

I also clearly recall my own delusional and confused thinking from the days before I wrote the Freedom Programme. I colluded with abusers in my role as a Probation Officer and put countless women in danger, because I had no understanding of how abusive men think and function. Since 1998, I have radically changed my views, and have reached some very different conclusions.

2

For example, there is no such being as an 'abused woman'. We are not a breed apart and we do not live in a bubble. We are not in abusive relationships because we are stupid, evil, alcoholic, poor, ill educated, mentally ill, unemployed or drug users. We are from every social, professional and economic group. We do not know that we are being abused. Therefore, we do not know that our children are being abused. We do not make the connection between their behaviour and the man in our life. Why should we? No one else does.

Many professionals involved in the child protection industry do not have this information either. Many blame women for deliberately colluding with abusers. A social worker who trained in America told me that she was taught to believe that there is a certain kind of woman who is attracted to abusers. Others collude unknowingly with the abuser just as I used to do. At some time in the last year or so, I answered the phone to a social worker who was trying to refer a man to one of my men's weekends. I occasionally provide these for men who 'want to become nicer men'.

The conversation went something like this:

> "I want to tell you his history."

> "I don't want to hear it. I will take any man as long as he behaves. I would accept Jack the Ripper as long as he does as he is told!"

> "No, it is not like that. He was so dreadfully abused by his first wife that he ended up serving a sentence for manslaughter. When he came out, he met a new girlfriend who was really nice. When she became pregnant, we completed a risk assessment for the baby and because she was so pleasant and they seemed so happy that we judged the risk to be low. He recently lost his temper, lashed out and hit her. He is really sorry and is desperate for help to control his temper."

> "Is his current victim attending the Freedom Programme?"

3

"Yes she is."

"He is very welcome to attend my weekend. However, before he comes he must read my book called 'Living with the Dominator'.

"No. He is not a Dominator. He is a lovely man."'

A lovely man! Really? He killed his first wife and attacked his second and he is lovely? I am not blaming that social worker. I was just the same when I was completely in the dark about how abusers operate. She is not unique.

Other social workers and family workers have been trained to use 'Solution Focused Therapy' with mothers who do not appear to be capable of parenting their children. SFBT targets the desired outcome of therapy as a solution rather than focusing on the symptoms or issues.

In this book, you will read accounts written by women who have been subjected to brutal physical violence and extreme emotional and psychological abuse. If any of them encounters one of these 'therapists' they will be invited to imagine how their lives could be improved and then consider ways of achieving this outcome.

In their situation, this 'intervention' is meaningless gibberish. If a child is then injured or murdered, the women who have already endured all this torture are then very likely to be convicted of causing or allowing the death of the child.

Dame Elizabeth Butler-Sloss is another person who believes that women collude with their abusers. She was the president of the High Court's Family Division. In the House of Lords, on 27.01.12, she said: *"Many women prefer the man to the child. She may, or may not, have committed the offence; much more likely is that she is covering up because the man is her support-financially and in every other way and, when faced with the choice between a man and a child,*

4

again and again, in my experience, the woman has chosen the man."

I completely disagree with that statement. When we women are in an abusive relationship we are not in a position to make any informed choice. We are completely controlled. We are brainwashed by the abuser and we do not know that he is damaging our children. Most women who have been sent on the programme by social workers tell me that, initially, they had no idea why they were there.
The Dominator effectively hypnotises his victims and unless we have done the Freedom Programme we have no idea what is happening. Many of those who offer professional help are also being abused but they do not know it. This woman victim is also a barrister.

Mail Online – 2 November 2011

Wife attack Judge James Allen sacked

A deputy high court judge who hit his wife during a row has been sacked for bringing the judiciary into disrepute.

James Allen QC was given a 12-month supervision order by District Judge Daphne Wickham after being convicted at Bradford Magistrates Court in June.

A spokeswoman for the Office for Judicial Complaints confirmed on Wednesday that 61-year-old Allen had been removed from his post.

During the trial Allen claimed his wife inflicted injuries on herself. She backed up his story. Mrs Allen is also a trained barrister.

One of the firsthand accounts that I have included in this book describes a situation where a serial abuser was cohabiting with two women simultaneously. One was a social worker and the other a teacher. Both bore him children.

5

We women are also constantly being told by the media and the judiciary that we are letting our children down by being single parents. The following recent quote is a prime example.

BBC News - 1 May 2012

By Katherine Sellgren BBC News education and family reporter

> *The breakdown of marriage is one of the "most destructive scourges" in modern UK society, says a High Court Judge. Sir Paul Coleridge is so concerned about family breakdown that he has launched a campaign to champion marriage as the 'gold standard for relationships'.*

If Sir Paul were to about read some of the marriages described in this book he may not be quite so complacent.

It seems to me that we women who attend the Freedom Programme and who join our online community are living in a parallel universe. I hear the Government talking about 'troubled families' and then I think of the 'trouble' we experience when living with a Dominator. I want to shout "Wake up! This is what is actually happening to us and to our children. Why can't you see it?"

It is hardly surprising that we are confused. We are blamed for staying and we are blamed for leaving. If we are religious, there is even more pressure on us to stay in dangerous relationships.

Claire Moore from Certain Curtain Company says:

> *'Instead of asking, why doesn't she just leave? People should be asking, why doesn't he just stop?'*

However, the fact remains that the only person who can save the lives of vulnerable and abused children is their mother. No one else has the power to make the changes that are desperately needed. We, as

6

freedomprogramme@btinternet.com   www.freedomprogramme.co.uk

mothers, can only make these changes when we are given information. We need to recognise and name abusive tactics. We need to understand exactly why abusive men want to control women and we must be told exactly how our children are affected. We also need to learn how their lives will improve after the Dominator has gone.

We can get this information from the Freedom Programme.

We also need to be aware that the danger to ourselves and our children can become more acute when we leave the relationship. At the very end of the book, in a sort of appalling appendix, I have added a list of quotes from press reports about men who have killed children as an act of revenge against the woman who is trying to leave them. This is a reminder, to anyone who blames women for failing to protect their children by staying with the abuser, of the danger we face when we try to leave.

Ironically, in western society, the media and Government appear to ignore this. We call it 'Honour Killing' when it happens in Asian families, but seem afflicted by selective blindness when it happens to our relatives and neighbours who are not Asian.

The main body of this book is based upon the section in the Freedom Programme that deals with the effects of domestic abuse on children. I have divided children in to three categories. The first group is comprised of a pregnant woman, an unborn child and a newborn baby. The second group is made up of children who are around six years old. The third group is teenagers. All these chapters include firsthand testimonies from women and children that illustrate how each group is affected. I also include some other personal stories as short chapters, which are complete in their own compelling way.

The final part of the book, before the appendix, is the most important and optimistic. This focuses on the improvements we can make for our children when we encounter the Freedom Programme and remove the Dominator from their lives. We face great difficulties, but we can make a difference if we know what can be achieved.

Chapter 2 – Pregnancy

'A woman is three times more likely to be injured when she is pregnant.' (Refuge 2007)

When I ask the abusive men who attend my courses why this may be the case, they have given me some very interesting answers. They said: *'She is fat and ugly', 'She is hormonal' (This implies it is her fault). 'Well you don't use violence until you have got your feet under the table do you? Clearly when she is pregnant you can get away with it.'*

When we are assaulted, they usually kick the unborn child and the baby can die. However, most of us do not make the connection between being assaulted and miscarrying. Sometimes, we realise years later when we are away from the Dominator and are attending the Freedom Programme.

This was written by Orchid

...My ex husband more than likely caused my baby's death. I woke up at 38 weeks pregnant at 8.30 am in absolute agony. I kept getting up and passing out. When I was unconscious, he dragged me back to bed. Since it first started I was pleading with him to call for help but he refused. I thought I was in labour and I was in no position to get help. He kept saying, 'You will be in trouble if there is nothing wrong'.

I didn't know then, but I was dying. Two hours later, at 10.30, he called the ambulance and, as he did so, he said, 'This had better be important'. When the ambulance arrived, he didn't come with me. The paramedics put on the flashing blues and took me to the delivery suite. They got a portable monitor and told me my baby was dead. I was taken for a crash section. I had a placental abruption.

8

I woke up on HDU in the delivery suite with tubes and wires coming out of me. The section had taken four hours and my little girl weighed 7lbs 1oz. I was told, after that, my blood pressure was 80/20 and that my blood count was five. I had a transfusion and they were going to do a hysterectomy that night if things didn't improve. They removed a blood clot from inside that weighed 450 grams.

I was told afterwards that my child could have been revived if I had got help immediately and not been delayed by two hours. They said I had been so close to death that my BP was in my boots. I was 23 years old.

This same husband had previously strangled me, beat me at 27 weeks in a previous pregnancy and used to sexually assault me on a regular basis. My elder kids don't know him. My daughters never want to meet him. They don't know what happened in detail but they know he was violent...

Dahlia

.... I attended three day training with you in 2011. With that, and reading everyone's messages on the forum, I have found I want to deal with my demons. It has been years since I suffered horrendous abuse from my husband and ended up in hospital on more than one occasion. I have never talked to anyone about what I went through. Now, after having worked in a women's refuge as a support worker for the last 10 years, I am suddenly experiencing flashbacks and often think of those bleak times in my life. After seeing you are writing a book with women's experiences, I wondered if there is anything I can help you with from what happened with me.

9

I was newly-married and fell pregnant with my first baby and couldn't get over the slap I got from my husband for not doing something how he wanted. I was stunned, but soon forgave him after listening to the excuses he gave about why it had happened (I was more gullible in those days!). This soon became another slap, and so on. I was about four months pregnant when he started to argue with me when we were in the street walking home. He pushed me then dropped me like a sack of potatoes on the ground. I went down with such a force, and landed square on my bottom. A sharp pain seared through my body. I got up, he laughed and we went home. That evening I started to bleed and had pains in my stomach. The doctor advised bed rest but nothing worked. My baby died, I ended up in hospital and had an operation to remove what was left.

That was one of the most horrendous moments I ever went through amongst all the other things. I didn't realise at the time it was connected to domestic abuse. It was only after being a support worker and coming on the training and running the Freedom Programme that I realised, if he hadn't dropped me to the ground, my baby may have not died. Before this, I had never made the connection between the domestic abuse I suffered and the loss of my baby.

I don't know if I have explained it very well, but I have found, as soon as I start to type about incidents, I get lost and it all seeps out. I have held all this in for so long...

Daisy

...We had been trying for a baby. We were having a row, don't know what about. He dragged me off the bed and along the landing and was going to throw me down the stairs and out of the house. I escaped and ran back to the bedroom.

10

I didn't know I was pregnant at the time and then, three weeks later, I had a miscarriage at seven weeks gestation. I look back now and think maybe he caused that. Of course, I will never know for sure and, at the time, I justified his behaviour by saying, 'Well, he didn't know I was pregnant'. But we were trying for a baby, and you don't do that to someone you are trying to have a baby with.

When I was seven months pregnant, he threatened to shut me up by smacking me in the face. I always felt that he wasn't violent toward me when I was pregnant, but I think I just decided to forget the times he was violent with me out of a kind of survival thing. I was too worried about being on my own with a baby, so I stayed with him despite the violence throughout all my pregnancies...

Babies who have been assaulted in the womb can be damaged and suffer from epilepsy or cerebral palsy.
As mothers, we very rarely make this connection…

Bluebell

…My dad kicked my mum in the stomach and assaulted her in many ways and I was born with a hole in my heart, and it made me very weak and small as a child and I missed a lot of school as I was always in hospital. I was always the smallest and weakest throughout my childhood and got bullied for being like that. Then, as an adult, I fell for abusers, so maybe I could say thanks to my dad for that sort of life....

Dominators refuse to let us rest when we are pregnant.
They do not help us to look after our other children and make continuous sexual demands.

Rose wrote this, with hindsight, after she had completed the Freedom Programme:

.....This was my situation when I was pregnant, and still with the Dominator. I remember what it was like for me.

I am stressed and have high anxiety. This is being passed to my unborn child. I had four miscarriages before having my first son. A cause was never found. I keep bleeding. I am so scared that I will lose this baby too.

I feel hideous. I hate being pregnant. He calls me fat and ugly. I don't look after myself correctly. I can't afford to eat enough healthy foods because he keeps all the money. I am scared if this baby will be healthy. I am sure my baby will be underweight.

I hardly sleep and I am so tired. I have to keep him company all night and massage his feet. I keep making mistakes the next day because I'm tired. I feel like I'm going mad, so I keep going to the doctors for depression.

I can't rest at all because he won't help look after the other children. How will I manage with another child? I don't think I want it. Will I love this baby?

I am pushed out of the bed to sleep on the floor and it hurts my back. My baby can hear all the noise and he becomes so unsettled in my stomach.

I am worried whether my baby's organs will be OK. I drink to forget about the affairs he keeps having. I want to stop, but I can't face my life.

I get locked out the house late at night with no clothes on. I keep getting chest infections...

This is an excerpt from the forthcoming Autobiography of
John Woudberg - **'Autobiography of a White Rat':**

...Three things about Mary

*They were lawless times. It was a lawless place; a place of
summary violence and crime; of spilled blood and beer in
the bars and murders unsolved; a place where the police
never came and where the words 'domestic violence' held
no meaning. It was dockland life, in a northern town,
in the late 1950s - closer in outlook and conditions to the
Victorians then we could ever imagine - as remote from
today as the earth from the moon.*

*It is 1959. I am six years old. I live with my mother in my
grandparents' cockroach-infested two-up two-down, in a
short terrace. In one of these slums lives Mary, a young
woman with a daughter my age. Mary lives there with her
mother and partner Danny. There are no airs and graces.
People just call out and walk into our house. Even the rag-
and-bone-man gets a cup of tea. Mary is always coming
round. She calls my grandmother Aunty Agnes, even though
she's not related. I play with her daughter, Sylvia, and I
overhear whispered things.*

*Three things about Mary my young eyes see. She always
has black-eyes. Swollen, purple 'shiners', almost shut.
"Danny was drunk again aunty," she murmurs, "He always
lashes out when he's drunk."*

*"He's a bad bastard," my grandmother replies, sipping her
tea. "You need to get shut of that bugger."*

*And so it goes - every black-eye, every visit - Danny and his
violence. The second thing my young eyes see is that Mary
is always pregnant. But when people ask her when is it
due? She goes crazy. "I'm not fucking pregnant," she cries.
"So just mind your own bloody business!"*

The third thing about Mary my young eyes see is ...no babies... She's pregnant - She's not - but only Sylvia comes round to play.

It is 1960 and Mary is pregnant again but no baby comes and Mary moves away. I sit playing on the cold lino and overhear whispered things. How Mary's mother had called out and walked in. How she swore my grandmother to secrecy. How Mary's pregnancy had gone full-term. How Danny had smothered the new-born and put its body in the fire. I think of the other babies.

They were lawless times. A place where the police never came and where the words 'domestic violence' held no meaning - as remote from today as the earth from the moon?...

freedomprogramme@btinternet.com   www.freedomprogramme.co.uk

Chapter 3 – The newborn baby

Dominators dictate how we give birth. If they are surgeons or consultants they may insist that we have caesarean sections even though there is no medical reason for it. They prevent us from breastfeeding or force us to do so against our will. They cut or break stitches to force us to have sex. They lock us out of the room when the baby is crying to be fed or changed. They say that this teaches the baby discipline.

Daffodil

> *..I would wake up hearing my son scream and cry, and when I opened the bedroom door to get to him (we lived in a bungalow), my ex would suddenly appear from a different room as fast as lightning and not allow me to get into my son's room, or he would be in there and at the bedroom door blocking my way...*

They use violence if we pick up the baby to play with it or cuddle it. This means that, to protect the baby, we ignore it.

Daffodil continues

> *...We agreed to split, but agreed to stay in the same house to look after our disabled child. I was totally controlled, emotionally, but didn't know it. I felt it but didn't understand. I kept repeating in my head, he's a good father. I was trying to make it true because the other option was unthinkable.*
>
> *If I didn't play by his rules, his punishment to me was to stop me seeing my child. When we were together, it was not being allowed to say goodnight or put him to bed. Even if my son was crying for me, I used to just sit there, as the last time I tried to get to him, my ex dropped my child on the floor, at no older than six months, and wouldn't pick him up until I left to sit down in the lounge. I carried that guilt, and saw him use that threat, time and time again.*

My son learnt to be quiet and to crawl into a space that only I could get to him and his father could not. It is only now that I am putting together some of my child's behaviours and where they originate from...

This can have a dreadful effect on the rest of this child's life. If they are never picked up, cuddled and hear loving words they do not know that they are lovable or even likeable. They may go through life without even knowing this is missing, but having no sense of self worth. How can they?

Rose remembers, after Freedom

....He controls and keeps the money. I can't afford to buy a pram or clothes or nappies. I can't ask anyone because I don't want anyone to think badly of him. My baby will just have to make do with the little I have.

The baby is so fretful and cries all the time. I have to keep him close to me all the time.

He won't let me attend to the baby when he cries. When I try to be with him, he says the baby must learn. My baby is feeling insecure and unsettled.

I can't breastfeed my baby because he says they are his boobs.

He wakes the baby up once I have finally settled him. Baby is confused and frightened.

There is no routine for the baby. I spend all my time running after his father and I just can't manage it all.

I find it hard to bond with my baby because he spends time with my mother to keep him safe. I want my baby in bed with me but I'm not allowed.

I do everything for the baby and the other children. He does

16

nothing at all. He has never changed one nappy.
I am shattered and the baby does not get the stimulation
he needs.

I am so scared when he is mad that I panic and try
everything to get my baby to sleep, but my baby panics too.

I have no money for the gas card for hot water so I can't
bath my baby.

The only toys my baby has are from his grandparents. Most
get broken...

Dominators also kill and injure babies.

Serious Case Review – Baby Peter

In spite of efforts by ambulance and hospital staff to revive him, Peter was pronounced dead at 12.10 pm. On initial examination, he was seen to have bruising to his body, a tooth missing, a torn frenum and marks to his head.

The Police Individual Management Review (IMR) referred to a post mortem completed on 6th August 2007 which revealed further injuries (a tooth was found in Peter's colon and eight fractured ribs on the left side and a fractured spine were detected). The provisional cause of death was described as a fracture / dislocation of the thoraco-lumbar spine.

A significant deficit in the first intervention with the family, which was then perpetuated, was the failure to establish the identity of Mr H, interview him and conduct checks on his background. He was the friend that Ms A claimed was peripheral to the family and had no involvement with the children. One of the most potentially dangerous scenarios in child protection is an unrelated man joining a vulnerable single parent family...

Orchid says

...Can you please also include something about a partner who always leaves a relationship and returns when he feels like it? He is using emotional abuse. A lot of us on the forum have been repeatedly subjected to this tactic. It makes us vulnerable which also hurts the kids. The worst possible time is when we are pregnant, giving birth or in poor health. They never give any reason. My ex did all this but before I joined the Freedom Programme Forum it would never had occurred to me that this was abuse.

Hubby Number Two was the love of my life and he was the one who played with my head. We were friends for two years before we got together. He was sweet, kind and lovely. We both lived up North and I was moving to Essex. We had got together and he moved in with me. The signs were there but I didn't realise.

He went to work one day and phoned me up and said we were finished. He changed his mind that evening and I put it down to a wobble. Around this time I discovered I was pregnant. He proposed and talked me into going back up North, which I did. I remember him not letting me read a magazine, he'd always read over my shoulder, I couldn't roll over in bed without him thinking I had the hump with him.

We got married and when I had the baby it got worse. He left two weeks after I had a c-section because I'd ask him to help me feed the baby. He came back after eight days. He left five times in four months. At the time, my older children were five and six and he was damaging them. He tried to remove the baby from my care, so I had to call the police. The signs were there but I didn't realise. He also threw me on the sofa in front of the girls.

18

On one occasion, he drove round the roundabout eight times. He had been shouting and I told him I wasn't going to respond if he was shouting. He pulled over on the dual carriageway, took the baby in her car seat, abandoned me, and the car, and walked off with her. I was shocked. I had no phone, keys or money and couldn't drive at the time. I had to wait 20 minutes for him to come back.

Then, one day, he'd asked my girls to put their pram away. They didn't respond quickly enough so he hit them round their heads. I didn't know until the next day. I'd slept on the sofa as I was restless. He came in the next morning and started shouting, 'Why didn't I want to sleep with him etc?'

Then the kids told me about him hitting them. He spent the whole of that day shouting, and I ended up telling him to leave. He'd previously left me for silly reasons, from the wrong shopping to him not taking me to the doctors after the baby's birth.

I'd had enough, and was isolated where we were because it was a little village where I didn't know anyone. I phoned a refuge and they got me a place back where I was, before, in Essex. I then filed for divorce. He refused to see the baby. He and his mother cut contact and he refused to answer his phone…

Social workers and police can become involved and babies can be removed.

Orchid (continued)

…I then lost custody of the kids, as my eldest, who I was carrying when I was assaulted in pregnancy, has extreme behavioural problems. I couldn't obtain help and she was

placed in residential specialist home. I fought to get the other two back.

I went through all the assessments and he (Orchid's husband) decided he wanted custody of the baby. It had already been decided that she was coming to me and was only a week away from being home full-time. He'd also had a child with someone else and they got back together to try to get my child.

During the court process, he didn't know my address at all. I had only been in the refuge three months and got a council house. He had no clue where it was. My solicitor raised it with the judge for my address to be withheld and it was agreed but they still included it in a court bundle, yet denied doing it. My legal team was furious.

He was awarded three hours per month access, minimum, and to be at my discretion where and when. I got a residency order as he tried to take her. We got back together and, after three months, he left again, just before I had major spinal surgery.

He kept leaving and coming back. Through counselling, I started to realise I had to stop this, or I was going to lose the kids. He left me up the pub and drove off and I had to make my own way home. I then found him packing, and this time I'd had enough.

We got back together when I was 26 weeks pregnant as he had been coming down once a month, and had been putting on the charm, trying to get his feet back under. I was ill and just went with it.

He was OK until the baby was three days old, then the shouting started. I was ill and he refused to take me to the

20

hospital. When she was 10 weeks old, he went again. All these times he left he never gave much notice. On one occasion, the kids and I were upstairs and hadn't known. I thought, at the time, that for a six-year-old to wake up and find her dad gone is heartbreaking. Now she says he's mean and asked if she could have a new dad!...

Dominators also use the legal system and other agencies to abuse us and damage their children.

Lavender

...When people consider abuse, and its effect on children, they are probably thinking about kids between the ages of three and 15. I think babies are the 'forgotten victims' in these situations due to their perceived lack of understanding. My experience has taught me that, although babies do not have the intellectual capacity to process the events going on around them, they are definitely affected by the atmosphere.

When my daughter was born she was a VERY discontented baby. She would constantly cry and was always unsettled. Being a first time mother, I simply just put her behaviour down to lack of routine. I thought she was hungry, colicky, teething or just being a newborn. Not once did it occur to me that she was picking up on the horrific vibes between her father and me. When she would cry my first instinct was to give her my breast, then check her nappy and then give her a cuddle. I became frustrated and felt inadequate as a mother when, at times, none of these things worked. I just could not work her out and would look at her in absolute desperation thinking, "What do you want from me?"

"What am I doing wrong? Why can't I make you happy?" Ironically, these are the very questions I would often ask her father!

I left my ex-partner when my baby was just 13 weeks old after he attacked me whilst I held her in my arms. I left the flat we shared in the heavy snow, with no money, the clothes on my back and just her changing bag, but it was the best decision I have ever made. My daughter was like a different baby when we left. She was so happy and content. The crying stopped and she was no longer jumpy. When we lived with her father, his mother remarked on how jumpy she was all the time. Admittedly, I do feel guilty that her first three months in the world were so unhappy, but I truly underestimated the effect it was having on her. I never understood properly until I witnessed the positive change in her behaviour once we had left. I'm just glad I made the break for both our sakes. Now I can provide her with the loving home environment she deserves.

The reason I left my ex-partner was because I did not ever want my child to bear witness to his despicable behaviour, I never ever wanted her to feel scared or confused in the crossfire of any violence. I am the product of a violent home and witnessed horrible things that are etched in my memory permanently. I wanted better for my daughter, which is why I got out when I did.

That dream has been shattered by the legal system, as my daughter has been emotionally abused as a result of being caught in the middle of an attack on me by my ex-partner. Her father attacked me during an ordered visit, and my daughter wet herself in fear. He marked my face and, as a result, my two-year-old baby was scared of me and would not cuddle me for a week. She would reject my affections and would just stare and point at my face. We have an exceptionally close bond, so this was a shattering experience for us both. It turned our world upside down for weeks whilst my daughter tried to process the trauma she witnessed in her poor little confused mind. I will never get back those precious moments that we lost, and I hold the

22

courts accountable for us being forced into harm's way in the first place.

My father was violent towards my mother, and she ended the relationship when I was four years old. I am now 27 and have vivid memories of the chaos I witnessed as a child. One of my memories was of me sitting on the edge of the sofa, staring at the sea of broken glass that covered the living room floor. I vaguely recall a space next to the fridge that was full of bottles which I now know to be wine bottles. My memory has images of the bottles suddenly not being there one day and the carpet covered in glass. I also remember being in bed ad seeing shards of glass next to me.

As an adult today, if I hear a glass smash I completely freak out. I once dropped a glass at home and when it smashed on the floor, I instantly burst into tears. It took me ages to muster the courage to sweep it up.

I made the mistake of confiding in my ex-Dominator about my childhood experiences and he listened attentively and comforted me whilst I poured my heart out to him about the things I witnessed. Little did I realise that, in true Dominator style, he was storing the information for future reference, as one day during an argument he took a glass and dangled it in front of me, threatening to smash it on the floor if I didn't comply with what he said.

Recently, my mother and I were talking and I told her about one of the other memories I have of my father throwing a meal she had prepared against the fridge in a rage. I told her I remembered the gravy slowly slithering down the front of the door. She was very shocked that I remembered something that happened 23 years ago when I was so young...

The next story provides a clear example of the way an ill-informed adviser can put women and children in danger. Daisy was trying so hard to follow the advice from a 'professional' who had no understanding of abusive men. I hate to think how many other women have been placed in her situation.

Daisy

.....Here are some of my experiences about the impact on the children. Much of the text is copied word-for-word from my journals at the time. When I first thought about this task I didn't think I would have much to contribute, then memories kept coming back and there are pages of the stuff.

Monday 29th December 2008

Poor Abigail, I worry for us both. She is so precious. The other day, he was in a mood and followed us up the stairs and deliberately left the stair gate open. I know he did it on purpose, how vindictive is that? He would wish harm upon her to get at me! Why? That is not normal. I hate being scared. I hate being threatened.

The next entry describes a very scary night when he locked me out of the house and I suddenly became sick with fear because my little girl was asleep inside.

I was terrified he would harm her to get at me. I left the house to get some space between us, as suggested by Relate Counselling, but after this experience I knew I could never leave the house again whilst my baby was in there. The fear of thinking something might happen to your child is very strong and it is a powerful way to control somebody.

24

Feb 28th 2009

He was shouting and then threatened me because I answered back. Lots of trigger points. Abigail's comforter was missing, the neighbour is giving him wood he now doesn't want, he was trying to watch rugby and, of course, he had been drinking. I was gradually being backed into the utility.

I asked several times for one of us to leave room as it was escalating. He said, "You leave" so I said, "Okay one of us needs to leave the house so the situation calms down. I'll do it".

I went to sit in the car. I could see he had turned all the lights off downstairs. I then panicked about Abigail. I thought, "What if he went to hurt her to spite me?" I'm sure he wouldn't, but I was really scared. I sat and cried in the car and, after five minutes, I tried to get back in the house. He'd locked the back gate and left keys in front door so I couldn't get in there, either. He has done this before and I've gone round the fields, climbed over a fence and got in the back door. I looked for torch, but it was not in the usual place. I thought, "Okay I'll give him a chance to open front door".

He opened it but said he wouldn't let me in. His face was full of anger and I was really frightened. I'm upset now writing it down, but he eventually let me in. We then had a discussion where I didn't really get a fair chance to speak and was belittled and patronised as usual. Before I left the house, he had told me not to speak, then asked me a question that required me to answer yes. I was scared to speak, so I didn't. He then said, "You can nod your head". Later in the argument, he said my head nodding was aggressive!!! .....

25

If this man had murdered Abigail while Daisy was locked out of the house she could have ended up in prison for failing to protect her daughter. The worker who gave such potentially lethal advice would not have faced any sanctions at all!

freedomprogramme@btinternet.com   www.freedomprogramme.co.uk

Chapter 4 – Six years old

Studies of children aged between the ages of one and six show that if someone plays with them, talks to them, reads to them and sings to them, they are more successful at school than children who have been ignored.

As the Dominator has ensured that we have been unable to interact with our children, they may start school at a disadvantage from which they may never recover. The Dominator has, effectively, forced us to ignore them for their own safety and to placate him.

Children need role models because we all learn by example. Our children do, indeed, have a role model. They can watch a giant baby having tantrums to get his own way. They can clearly see that this tactic is successful, so they copy it in nursery or school. They can be excluded and then we take them to the doctor who can often diagnose ADHD.

I want to stress that, as a mother in this situation, I do not make the connection between the influence of the Dominator and the behaviour of my child. I visit the doctor in good faith and I gratefully accept the diagnosis. This is clear from the narratives we have included in this book.

There can also be another factor at work here. If a child is smacked for displeasing an adult, then they are being given a clear message. The message is that it is acceptable to assault someone who has done something you do not like. This lesson can also last a lifetime.

Children of any age need friends. Friends can teach us how to behave socially, to play, communicate and share. This is a way to practise how to behave for the rest of our lives. Dominators are Jailers who do not allow anyone into the house. They cannot bring friends home. Soon, other children do not invite our young children to visit or play. Children of the Dominator have no friends.

27

The absence of friends can affect our children in another deeply damaging way. Friends can show us affection. They can say, "I like you", "I want to be your friend". Young children who have been ignored by their mother to keep them safe cannot get any affection from anywhere else.

Children can also get a lot of stimulus and love from their extended family. The Jailor has also excluded aunts, uncles, grandparents and all their mother's friends. No one is there for our six-year-old. No one shows them any love.

Rich Dominators also send our children away to boarding school from a very early age. They convince us, and everyone else, that this is an advantage to the child. I am not the only person to challenge this notion.

George Monbiot, guardian.co.uk, Monday 16 January 2012

...The UK Boarding Schools website lists 18 schools which take boarders from the age of eight, and 38 which take them from the age of seven. I expect such places have improved over the past 40 years; they could scarcely have got worse. Children are likely to have more contact with home; though one school I phoned last week told me that some of its pupils still see their parents only in the holidays. But the nature of boarding is only one of the forces that can harm these children. The other is the fact of boarding.

In a paper published last year in the British Journal of Psychotherapy, Dr Joy Schaverien identifies a set of symptoms common among early boarders that she calls Boarding School Syndrome. Her research suggests that the act of separation, regardless of what might follow it, "can cause profound developmental damage", as "early rupture with home has a lasting influence on attachment patterns".

*When a child is brought up at home, the family adapts
to accommodate it: growing up involves a constant
negotiation between parents and children.
But an institution cannot rebuild itself around one child.
Instead, the child must adapt to the system. Combined with
the sudden and repeated loss of parents, siblings, pets and
toys, this causes the child to shut itself off from the need for
intimacy. This can cause major problems in adulthood:
depression, an inability to talk about or understand
emotions, the urge to escape from or to destroy intimate
relationships. These symptoms mostly affect early boarders:
those who start when they are older are less likely
to be harmed....*

George Monbiot is wrong to assert that children are accepted from the age of seven. I have just done an internet search and found several schools who accept children as young as three!

Young, growing children need regular nutritious meals to help them to grow and develop. They also need to learn to eat in the company of others. When the Dominator is in charge, mealtimes are fraught with tension and fear. I am reminded of the occasion when I asked a group of men this question: "What happens at mealtimes in the home of the Dominator?" Several gave this answer, "The food goes up the wall." As though it flies up there of its own volition! However, one man who had learned a lot from my teaching said, thoughtfully, "In my house I used to throw it at 'woman height' so she could clean it up quickly." The others then nodded in agreement. I include this story to remind us all that the Dominator is never angry and plans every move in advance.

Children in this situation can associate food with fear and tension. They can develop eating disorders. They can become too tense to eat, or may gobble or hoard food. All my associates who work in refuges have seen children who behave like this when they arrive, after fleeing from Dominators. Nearly every adult I know, who has problems with

29

food, grew up in a home where they were terrorised by a Dominator.

Our children need sleep at this age. They are growing fast and need to be alert during those vital early years at school. Sadly, they do not sleep. They lie awake in terror, listening to the noise and violence downstairs. They may wet the bed. In the morning, we hurry them from the house to avoid the wrath of the Dominator. We may not have the time to clean and tidy them so we may take them to school unkempt and smelly.

This can happen in any social group. A friend told me that her father was a consultant paediatrician, and this is exactly what happened to her. When she went to school she had no friends to protect her, she was not thriving in class and was bullied mercilessly.

Once again, as the mother, we fail to make the connection between the bed wetting and the Dominator, and we take our child to the doctor for yet more medication!

Rose again:

...My oldest son said, a few days ago, "Remember when me and you slept in the car mum? The little green car?"

I am amazed that he could remember, he was so young.

"Remember, mummy, when dad used to play the banister game? He would take us to the top of the stairs and hold us over the banister, dangling us, you used to scream and cry and tell him to stop but he wouldn't.

"OUR LIVES ARE SO MUCH BETTER NOW MUMMY."

My teenage son said to me the other day, "Mum I remember when dad bought me new trainers and they did not fit. I was too scared to tell him, so I wore them too small."

Rose's nine-year-old daughter

... "When we lived with dad, mum was always upset and sad. That made us sad. Dad used to throw the food at the wall, because nothing was ever good enough for him.
It was like we never got to see mum because dad was always shouting at her. Well, apparently, he was talking, but who was born yesterday? He used to hang us over the banister, we used to scream and shout but he wouldn't stop. Life is better now we don't live with dad. Life is better now because we are happier, not sad. No one throws stuff at the walls. No one shouts and gets bullied...

Rose's 11-year-old son

Living with my dad was hard. I used to get really scared and frightened of him. He used to hit mummy and I had to see it all the time. What usually happened was that they would argue and mum would cry. They would go into the front room and dad used to tell us to go upstairs. I used to hear banging and dad's voice saying nasty things. Mum would scream. Next, dad would tell us to come down and say to us that he was sorry and mum was being nasty and doing wrong things. Dad would go out and we didn't know where. He would come in drunk and hang us over the banister. We would cry and scream while mum would be crying. Eventually, we would go to bed but at about one o'clock or two he would wake me and my older brother up to watch 18s with him. We would be really tired the next day and nanny would get us up and ready for school and take us there. Dad would cheat on mum with other girls
and never actually come home without being drunk.

Clearly Rose's three children remember life with their father all too clearly.

Daisy
...Verbal abuse at bedtime

He would verbally abuse me when I was putting the children to bed. Literally, I would have the baby in my arms placing her in her cot, and he would start on me. I remember thinking how inappropriate it was, but didn't want to argue back or else I would be just as bad as him. All my children were fitful sleepers and never slept right through. Looking back I can see why, but at the time I never made the connection. Bedtime is supposed to be relaxed and calm, and yet here they are being put to bed whilst their mummy is being yelled at. I feel really sad that I let this go on for so long. Now I am free, I do wonder how much the four-year-old may have heard whist she was in bed, supposedly asleep. I worry she may have woken and heard him ranting at me. Was she frightened? How did she feel? It doesn't bear thinking about.

The night of his last attack on me I actually ran into Abigail's room at one point for protection. Yes, it was ridiculous, but I ran into a two-year year olds bedroom for protection. I just thought he would leave me alone if I was near her. She was asleep, but he still yelled, "Don't bring her into this, get out." So that was the end of that. Once his attack was over (it lasted several hours), and I could hear him sleeping in the spare room, I was tempted to sleep on the floor of Abigail's room to feel safer, but I didn't in case he caught me. I am very ashamed of this now, that I would think a two-year-old could protect me. I should have been protecting her.

32

Not being able to show love

This is really hard to explain, but I don't think I was able to show my love for my children properly when I lived with my abuser. Now I cuddle and tell them how much I love them so much more. I think, before, it was because they were a chore that had to be done, before I had to deal with him.

Throwing Rachel

Rachel was just one year old. Robert and I were at Abigail's birthday with my mother and stepfather. I left Robert with the two children and went to get some things from the car. When I returned he shouted at me for leaving him with "these two". At this point he threw Rachel at me, I stumbled backwards and my stepdad caught Rachel. I was so shocked that he would have an outburst like this in public, and then I just felt really scared about going home. I hadn't really registered that he had thrown our one-year-old across to me.

I think when you are in this kind of relationship you are so blinkered and so convinced that everything is normal that you don't see the harm that is going on around you. It wasn't that I didn't care about Rachel being thrown, I just couldn't think about it because now I was focusing on how I could placate him before we all got home alone with him...

Children need to be told the truth. They need the truth to make sense of their experience of the world. So when my child asks me, 'Why is daddy hitting you?' I am likely to respond in a variety of ways. If daddy is listening, as he so often is, I will deny that he did hit me. My child has just witnessed this, and now I am telling them that they cannot believe their own eyes. I may also say something like, 'daddy was only playing' or 'daddy is not well'. They may also hear daddy saying when he does hit me, 'I am only doing this because I love you'.

Clearly, this is sending children a message that if you love someone you hit them. There is no doubt that children and young people are accepting this distorted view of relationships.

Zero Tolerance Charitable Trust 1998

One in five young men and one in ten young women think that abuse or violence is acceptable.

Sugar magazine and NSPCC online survey (2005)

Teen Abuse survey of Great Britain

4% of teenage girls were subjected to regular attacks by their partner.

16% had been hit at least once.

31% thought that it was 'acceptable' for a boy to act in an aggressive' way if his girlfriend has cheated on him.

6% girls between 13-19, with an average age of 15, had been forced to have sex with their boyfriend, and 1 in 3 forgave him and stayed with him.

Bliss magazine and Woman's Aid online survey (2008)

One in four 16-year-old girls know of someone else who has been hurt or hit by someone they are dating.

One in six 15-year-old girls and more than one in four 16-year-old girls who took part in the survey (27%) have been hit or hurt in some way by someone they were dating.

When we finally escape from the Dominator he continues to abuse us and our children by enlisting the help of statutory agencies.

Daffodil continues her story:

...My ex started a campaign against me which was designed to get the house and for me to pay for it through child benefits etc. It had nothing to do with my child. He got a gullible social worker on his side. I did not realise the amount of emotional abuse he was using, and did not understand what was really happening. I fell in to his trap. My mother's phase was, "He loads the gun and then gets others to pull the trigger".

I started to be investigated on false allegations which were kept from me, and they used my mental health as the reasons. The stress was so bad at the house, I started to stay at work until my child was in bed asleep, believing that I was saving him by keeping him away from what was happening. I was not. He was picking it all up.

Just before I left, my parents came over for a week's holiday, which was well timed and good that I didn't go over to them as I was told by my solicitor and GP that, if I left the area, social services would go for an emergency application to remove my child as I was under investigation.

The holiday was without my ex. My son, at the start, again in my Mum's words, was like a wild angry animal, and all he would eat was one food type. By the end of the week, he was getting back to his normal, happier self. He was a child they would have been happy not to see again because of the behaviour. This was his 5th birthday week...

Later, after Daffodil's ex had assaulted her and been let off with a caution, the family courts ordered shared residence.

35

....So they split him [my son] 60-40 to me and, supposedly, 50-50 during holiday times. My son has stopped concentrating at school. He asks me not to go to daddy's. He says he loves him but doesn't want to spend so much time there.

My son stopped sleeping through the night, started having nightmares, especially if he was going to his father's. He started wetting himself, started taking his clothes off so he didn't get them dirty, asking for a nappy back on. He asks me, "When am I going to live with you?"

My child minder won't have my son on the day he comes from his father because he is exhausted, aggressive and whines for the first part of the afternoon. I have lost over 20% of my wage, so I have to work fulltime. I have arranged it so I see my son on two of the three afternoons I have him, and work long days the rest of the time.

After settling back in, my son almost lets out a huge breath and starts to relax and breathe and become a typical five-year-old. This lasts until he has to go back. The maximum we have, excluding holidays, is five nights, the shortest is three nights...

When the Dominator starts to build up to a violent episode, we mothers try to protect our children by getting them out of the way. We send them to their rooms or out to play in the street. Once they are there, they may join all the other children who have been sent out to escape from Dominators. Our children may join together to form gangs. They already have a lot in common, and they can start to abuse drugs and alcohol and to break the law.

Young children will also hear the Dominator call their mother vile names. Slut and slag are among the mildest of them. They will learn not to respect her or any women, even if they do not yet know what these words mean. Both boys and girls can share these beliefs.

Lily

...Looking back during our time with our Dominator, my son's behaviour (he was 10 when we left) was awful. He was physically violent and spiteful towards females. He had no respect for females and would often name call. Since we have been free, his behaviour has improved a million per cent. He is now 15 and he is a wonderful kid. My daughter, who was eight at the time, was clingy, nervous, shy and extremely manipulative. Now, at 14, she is confident and outgoing and naturally comical!! She still has the ability to wrap males around her little finger.

It was a long and painful journey to get my children to adjust their behaviour. They fought me all the way because they had spent so long behaving inappropriately, but we got there in the end.

My son broke my heart one day last year. He said to me, "I saw him beat you when he had you on the bedroom floor and I'm sorry". I asked him why he was sorry, and he said, "Because I didn't help you".

When my daughter was 11, she asked if she could learn karate. I asked her why, and she said, "Because WHEN a man beats me up I can defend myself. You should have done karate mummy, then you could have been the one to do the beating up, and you wouldn't have got hurt all the time".

Just because children don't tell you what they see, doesn't mean they haven't seen it...

Dominators scapegoat one child and spoil the others. They can pretend to love the scapegoat. They turn the children against one another. This can make it even more difficult when we are trying to leave the relationship.

Magnolia

...Peter was sitting next to me in the front seat of the car. My precious little boy, who I had sworn would never know abuse, didn't know what had hit him when I got together with Michael. He was three at the beginning of it all, and here we were three years later, sharing a very rare moment alone together. I knew I couldn't say too much, as bad mouthing Michael wasn't allowed, and I had to be careful in case Peter, unwittingly, repeated anything we spoke about. I put my hand on his leg and said, "Things will be better when we're away from Michael".

I felt so guilty that I'd exposed my baby to a man who hated him. I wasn't allowed to talk to Peter, except to tell him off, which I usually did to ward off any need for Michael to punish my son for crimes that Michael had made up. I couldn't cuddle him because I would be accused of not loving Michael's children and of having Peter as a favourite. The scapegoat stepchild had become a very angry little boy. Michael said Peter had always been like that, since he turned two, but I couldn't help thinking that Michael's endless criticism, relentless taunting and horrible physical abuse had shaped Peter's temper. Peter had no bond with his twin stepsisters. He showed no interest at all because he wasn't allowed to.

Peter looked up at me and said he liked Michael. I was horrified that he couldn't see what a nasty snake Michael was. He had only ever pretended to like Peter. Peter had even accepted that he had to wipe his mouth before he kissed his stepdad. Michael's children could kiss him, but he said

38

"Peter was a dribbler" to justify abruptly shoving his hand in Peter's face as he leaned in to say 'Goodnight'. I felt so trapped. I knew I had to get us out of there, but I could tell that Peter would feel I was depriving him of a daddy if I did…

Sunflower

…One of my early memories as an eight-year-old is being pinned to the wall with my father twisting my neck chain with a dangling 'Star of David' (symbol of Judaism) and choking me as he called me 'a fucking yid bastard', whilst my mother wrestled with him to get him off. He would eventually loosen his hold, leaving me weak and terrified, to slide down the wall and land with a thump. I was terrified, but always defiant. I would always threaten to get even, to call the police and get him sent to prison. He would laugh and look at me with contempt and disgust.

I did call the police. I called them often, in fact, but the domestic violence laws in the 1950s supported the principle that 'the man's home was his castle' and in his castle he 'could rule as he saw fit'. So he always won, and I spent my childhood living in a war zone, which I believed was 'normal'. My mother originated from Russian Jews who had fled Tallinn in the late 1900s to escape persecution. On a happy day in 1938 she had been ambling through Hyde Park in London, over the road from her home, when a good looking man in his Coldstream Guards uniform started to talk to her. He was handsome and charming. This Liverpool lad, of Irish descent, fitted her dream of a man to love. She certainly did love him! She loved him through terror, abuse, violence, betrayal and repeated abandonment.

*My problem was that I wanted my father to love me too.
I thought he did when he took me to Club Row in the East
End of London and paid 50p for the cutest puppy which I
named 'Fluffy'. The poor dog spent more time with my
father's hands round her throat while he dangled her out of
a third floor window from our Hackney council flat. Her
eyes would bulge with terror and I would be screaming as
he repeatedly threatened to drop her from the heights. He
would also return home after his many 'trips' away with
lavish gifts like a transistor radio, television or a record
player. Every time he did this I thought, 'He must love me'.
Within months, the bailiffs would be at the door demanding
that the goods be returned to the store. He had only left a
deposit with the promise of further hire purchase payments.
He would laugh at my torment!*

*As I result of all this chaos and trauma, I constantly wet
the bed and developed asthma, for which I was repeatedly
hospitalised. I was labelled a 'sick child'. My father
repeatedly told me it was from the bastard 'yid' side of the
family as such weakness could not stem from his healthy,
strong roots. Every year, I was sent away for a two-week
holiday to Cliftonville in Margate, Kent.*

*This charitable act, from the Jewish Board of Guardians,
was instigated by our local doctor 'to give my mother a
break from her sickly daughter'. I was bereft. Although I
was away from direct fear, I was terrified my mother would
die, that 'he' would kill her. I would constantly cry and tell
the people in charge to telephone her. They became sick to
death of me. They labelled me as difficult and calmed me
down with some sort of sedative. No one ever listened to
my fears!*

I would plan his death in my mind constantly. How I would kill him and how, then, we would be 'free'. In fact we became 'free' when I was around 15 years old and he finally left with his then current woman. He tried to return, but by this time I had met my own 'man of my dreams' who punched my father on his attempt to return to the family home and beat my mother. This 'man of my dreams' was one of two men I married. I prided myself that I had not followed my mother's pattern of abusive men, because after all I had never been hit! How wrong I was!

Chapter 5 - The Teenager

Children are frequently removed from their homes and placed in the care of the Local Authority. They are removed to protect them from violence, abuse and neglect. Today this was the headline on the BBC news website:

… The government has published plans to combat the sexual exploitation of children in care homes in England by gangs.

Teenagers can also end up homeless and living on the streets. They too are vulnerable to abuse and trafficking.

Orchid

…Twenty years ago, next month, my mother's boyfriend dragged me up the stairs by my hair, split my lip and chipped my teeth. My mother just sat there and carried on eating her dinner. My sister tried to help me, but was told not to come near me.

The next day, I went to school at 7am and my friend told the head teacher I'd been attacked, my lip was swollen, I had a black eye and bruises on my body.
The social services were called and I was interviewed all day by the police at the social services office. My mother had written a letter to say she no longer wanted me at home and had packed a bag of my belongings. I was taken into foster care. I had just turned 14.

My crime was going to the after school trampoline class. He'd previously kicked me in the stomach, insulted me, he used to go through my bedroom and I had no privacy.
I stayed in foster care, then in a children's home and, eight months later, my mother said she wanted me home. I pleaded with them not to send me.

I'd been home for three months and had been sitting on my bed. He came into my room and knocked me off my bed into a bookcase. I was taken back into care until I was 16, to the same children's home. My mother's boyfriend did not hit my mother until I was 18, when he put her in hospital. The minute he hit her she got rid of him.

Not once was I offered counselling. Nothing! I then, unsurprisingly, married two nasty men. I carried this with me until my first breakdown when my baby died...

Rose's son wrote about his life before his mother did the Freedom Programme and left his father. He wrote this with Rose's help.

Rose's son

...I am thirteen years old.

I have been expelled from school because when I do not get my own way I kick off like dad does at home.

I am afraid of other teenagers and people I do not know, I do not know who to trust.

Everything must be perfect at all times, I want to please dad.

I have no self-esteem, I do not like myself.

I have little social skills. I find it difficult to interact with other people.

I am three years behind in my school work because I missed so much school.

I am easily led. I just want to belong somewhere.

freedomprogramme@btinternet.com   www.freedomprogramme.co.uk

I hardly sleep, I have constant night terrors.

My mum has to sit with me till I fall asleep. I don't like falling asleep, I am frightened of what will happen because Dad is sure to kick off.

I hit, spit, shout and scream when I do not get my own way. It works for dad.

I smash things. Dad smashes things.

Peace Lily

...Last night my 13-year-old son, Sam, witnessed my partner hitting me. It's the first time he's hit me after mental abuse, and for my son to see it has rocked us to the core. My son has just had to make a two-hour statement at the police station saying what happened and what he saw.

Peace Lily's son Sam

My mum met Daniel on an Atlantic cruise. He sat on our dinner table with my mum, me and granny. He was very nice and made us laugh, and mum kept in touch with him. He started to come to our house every weekend because he lived far away.

Daniel used to annoy me because he used to cut me out, when I was with mum, and he would blame me for everything and open all the letters and check my mum's phone. He would come running though and ask, threateningly, "Care to explain?" and start quizzing us both. My mum would get angry and tell him to go, but he would walk out and then come back and upset us.

44

     freedomprogramme@btinternet.com   www.freedomprogramme.co.uk

I hated being at home when he was there, I wanted to move in with my dad but I knew mum would get upset. I didn't want to leave her because I was scared he would hurt her.

Daniel always said it was my fault, and when he did things wrong or broke things he would blame me. He broke mum's iron and blamed me. I got angry and he shouted at me and upset me. I told my dad and he shouted at Daniel on the phone and I just wanted to go.

I couldn't sleep at night because I could hear him picking on my mum and accusing the man around the corner of looking at her. The man was looking at my mum because she is pretty, and I told Daniel the man was cutting his lawn and looked and smiled at mum. He went mad and stormed out.

When he stormed out I was pleased because I hated him. But then he would come back, and I would say to mum, 'I don't want him here'. My mum said she had to move on and I wouldn't like any boyfriend, but I did. I liked Mike, who was mum's boyfriend before Daniel. Mum stayed friends with Mike because he was kind, but mum said he was ugly. Daniel stopped mum being friends with Mike, and Daniel deleted my garage on my Playstation because it said 'Mike's Place'. Mike had given me the game. I was upset because I lost all my cars and Daniel was jealous. But I couldn't get my cars back and I was really upset.

Once, on the boat, he was doing the lock and he was messing it up and mum was laughing and she was going to help him. He fell into the boat and blamed me. It wasn't my fault but he shouted at me, so I sat in the cabin all weekend and mum said I spoilt the weekend. It was Daniel, not me. He was moaning and blaming me.

I'm pleased Daniel never moved in with us, because I was always in the way. He hated me and he hated mum talking to

45

Mike. He deleted Mike's number and was always challenging mum. Mum would then shout and get stressed with me. Every time we were going to go out he spoilt it.

Then Daniel hit my mum in front of me and I had to tell the police what he did. I was really scared, because I thought he would hit me, so I rang my dad. My dad was really angry and said, 'It's about time your mum got rid of that idiot'. My mum is really upset and I hope he doesn't come back because it is so relaxed now and I can be with my mum without her being upset. I keep telling her she should get rid, and I hate him. I hope she listens now...

Rose

...Last night I worked night shift with my little sister. I have four sisters and three brothers. My father has had three wives, the first being my mother. He left her penniless and pregnant with me and my two older brothers. The marriage was full of mental, financial and emotional abuse.
My mother still talks very little of it.

He then took up another young wife who gave birth to my half sister. He had five additional children with her.
My sisters were bought up with two mothers. Both are professionals, a teacher and social worker, and both worked long hours whilst he gained degree after degree.
He never worked one day in his life. A Doctor of Psychology and Sociology and I would like to say a doctor of Bolloxology!

Two of my sisters, they are twins, ran away at fourteen. They never went back and ended up in my home town.
They both have now read the Freedom book and know how passionate I am about it. I asked them to contribute to the new book, but they both felt they were unable to because it was just too painful. However, I mentioned to one of them

last night at work that you were doing the final draft.

*She is now twenty two. It opened up a conversation;
this is how it went:*

"I can't remember anything honestly. It's just all blank."

*"Really are you sure? Did you not think it was strange that
Dad had two wives?"*

*"No I just thought it was normal. I knew other people didn't
do it, but it was still normal to me. I didn't realise it was
wrong. I don't think I cared about him. I didn't like him. I
hated it when I could hear him having sex with mum in the
room next door."*

She laughed. She uses humour in life a lot.

*"Tell Pat that dad did me a favour in a way. He used to
send me outside. I spent a lot of time on the balcony so I got
a good sun tan. Tell her I am obsessed with clothes because
we had none as children."*

"Do you think your mum is happy now she not with him?"

"God, she's still fucked up."

"You hated his bible readings didn't you?"

*"Bible readings! Ha! They were pathetic, chanting every
morning, chanting every night. I hated weekends, no TV, no
music, not allowed to see our friends from school. We had to
do long walks all the time, every weekend, up the hills, down
the hills, only talking to each other. I'm sure that's why I
love partying now."*

*Both girls are now twenty two. They ran away from home to
my town and, amazingly, social services put them with me! I*

was living with my Dominator at the time! They never stayed long. They both went into teenager runaway accommodation. Both ended up with abusive partners. One was heavily into drugs, but turned her life around when she had a child at nineteen. She ended her relationship and is about to start university! The other ended up living with my husband. He was just as awful to her as he was me. None of us talked to her for two years. I hated her! Until I read the Freedom book! I then begin texting her lines from the book daily. We all began to talk to her and she read the book. She left him!

All three of us are very close, we've all read the book.

Amazing how it all trickles out to so many people, forever grateful xxxxxxxxx

freedomprogramme@btinternet.com   www.freedomprogramme.co.uk

Chapter 6 - Poppy

Hi, Pat

…I signed up to the Freedom Programme forum a while back, but have never had the confidence to post anything. This is partly because writing things down makes the situations more real rather than some hazy nightmare. You can probably guess from that that I am in an abusive relationship at present.

I have only ever had four relationships and three were, or are, very abusive. I don't understand why I get it so wrong all of the time. I just believe people when they say they're going to love and look after me. I believe that's what they're going to do and not try to destroy me as a human being in every way they can. I am trying to get my head around ending this one now. I have found, with the other two, that circumstances gave me the opportunities to sort things. I'm not relying on that now, but I need to be 100% confident (or as best as I can be) to sort this, as I have to be strong for my children to manage their pain.

I have two very complex disabled children who both need round the clock 24 hour care. I have no family, as they disowned me when they found out I had disabled children. I was branded 'a failure'. My family had always been disjointed. My mother walked out when I was 13. My father didn't want my brother and me. My mother didn't want the stigma of having a child in care, so I lived with my mother and stepfather until I was 16. It was horrific. When I was 16, they left me alone in London where I got myself a job and a bedsit and was self-sufficient from then on. A lot of bad things happened throughout my childhood, but I was always determined to make a life for myself and not allow the bad things to rule my future.

Bringing things up-to-date, my ex-husband, who is the father of my children, was abusive to me and the children. Both of my children have autism, as well as other complex mental

49

disabilities and physical disabilities. For example, my son cannot walk properly. My son could not talk until he was about 3 ½ and, when he did, my ex-husband couldn't cope, so he would try and hold his hand over my son's mouth. One day, my son bit his daddy for holding his wrist so hard, so my ex bit him back. It got so bad I could not allow my ex to be alone with the children and our GP confirmed this when we went to see him.
I would have to take them to the toilet with me to wait outside so I knew they were safe.

At that time, I was fighting through the courts for my children to have a right to an education. I did this alone. My children were both backwards and forwards to hospital constantly. I also had become very seriously ill myself, to the point where I had to be tube fed and went down to six stone. My ex abused me verbally and I constantly encouraged him to keep away from the house, which he did do. An example of what we used to go through was how my ex could not cope with talking in the car at all.
My children, being disabled, do not understand that, so they would get it 'wrong' and break the rules.

One day we had to go and visit a new potential special school for my children. My ex got lost and his temper erupted.
He screamed in the car and drove like a mad man through the city streets. He was shouting how he was going to kill us. The children were terrified and so was I. The car screeched to a halt in four lanes of traffic. I was sat in the back with my son supporting him. I banged open my son's, my daughter's and my own seat belts. I shouted for my daughter to get out of the car and lifted my son out. Car seats were strewn across the road. We wove our way through the traffic to the pavement where strangers met a crying little family. Unbelievably, we were opposite the police station and they ran out to help. My ex crashed the car further up the road. Back then, the police did not offer us advice on refuges or support. We were expected to go home with my ex. Having no family and no money,
we had no choice.

Slowly, I began to realise things had to change, and I sought information and saved pennies until, one day, I told him to go, and he did. I should mention that my son, who was seven at the time, was very violent himself. He would pull my hair out, he split my lip open and I had to have four stitches. The scars are still there today. He scratched and punched. The day my ex left, my son's violence stopped! It was incredible. My little boy became the beautiful young person I always knew he could be and, despite all of his disabilities, he is one of the most caring, loving people I have ever known.

That is not the end of the story sadly. I did say, initially, my ex could see the children at home when he liked, providing he was good and kind to them. I explained how scared they were of him and how he had to work at regaining there trust. He visited twice and both times he was abusive, aggressive and distressed the children. So I went straight to a solicitor and she banned him from seeing the children. We had to go to court. That first session in court was terrifying. My children did not want to see their daddy. Had they done so, I would have agreed to him having contact which was supervised. I just wanted them to be happy. They were terrified and made it clear they did not want to see him again. I was the children's voice. But, at that first court hearing, the judge told me my children had no voice as they were children and disabled. So I fought hard for a year for the judge to understand they had a right to their views. After all, he was expecting them to spend time with a man who had used abusive behaviour, which was recorded by several professionals.

During that year, I was told I had to pay for my ex to see the children. I had to pay for the supervision. The supervisors had to be people the children knew and trusted. We also had the worst CAFCASS officer who had no idea of the children's disabilities and she confused them and upset them. She was exceptionally patronising and it was obvious she was on my ex's side.

During this time, I was also in court fighting for my children's right to have an education.

I won my daughter's case first and she started to attend a special school for autistic children. But the CAFCASS worker insisted that my daughter be removed from school twice a week to see her daddy, which I thought appalling considering she had been out of school for three years (that is how long the cases took to fight). I made a formal complaint about the CAFCASS worker and it was upheld and we were given a senior manager who was fantastic.

My ex also wanted to see the children on weekends. Considering he didn't show them any interest when he was at home other than to harm them, I knew this was just a game to him of hitting back at me. The supervised visits were horrendous for the children. Their dad still was abusive and things completely broke down when he assaulted my son in front of a supervisor in a park.

It was then that the judge sat up and ordered that the children be given a legal voice. They would have their own solicitor and a Guardian Ad Litem. I was so pleased. They spent time with the children and were brilliant in understanding them. They produced reports for court, dictated by the children, about their daddy. The pictures the children used, to show what they thought their daddy was like, were terrifying; a distorted face full of rage; broken furniture; angry bubbles with angry words in. The judge ordered that only indirect contact was allowed, via a specialised website.

My ex wanted the children to write three times a week. This was unrealistic, considering the fact neither of them could read nor write. Because of this, and their other disabilities, they needed so much time to process things and decide what they wanted to say. In the end it was ordered the children only had to write once every 4 weeks, but more if they wanted, and my ex could write every day, if he wanted to. I put in masses of effort to try and encourage the relationship, and the letter writing process, but their dad skipped some months, although the children always wrote. When they did get letters, their dad always wrote about himself and showed no interest in the children. After eight months, the case returned to court, where the judge ordered it to be closed. Their dad could not have access to the children, other than indirectly.

My ex wanted the case to remain open, so if he ever wanted to contest again he could and he wouldn't have to pay. The judge insisted this was not going to happen and said that, if he cared about his children that much, he would be happy to pay (my ex had a good job). Since that time, three years ago, the children have not heard from their dad, other than an odd birthday card with the wrong age written on. I have never said bad things about the children's daddy to them, they know what we have all been through and he is still their daddy. Also, I have always said to them if they want contact I would arrange for it to be supervised immediately if it was possible. But both remain steadfast they never want to see him again.

My current partner promised me the world, and instead he stole it from me.

We have been together four years. He is sly and underhanded, abusive and cruel to me. He has been verbally awful to the children at odd times, but this happens infrequently and my son loves him to bits. I think this is only because, when my partner rarely does spend bit of time with him, he feels so happy. I know I have to sort the mess out, and soon. I am able to hide a lot from the children, but I want things to stop now for all our sakes. I don't want the children subjected to anymore. I am aware that there is always the risk of them witnessing something or having some mean words thrown at them. The house is mine, and for that I am so grateful. My ex's name is on the mortgage too, but I pay for everything. So I can tell my partner to leave.

I thought he loved me. I thought he cared, but he doesn't. Before he moved in, when he met the children, he played with them on the floor and I thought, 'Wow! He is a real hands-on dad!' I have not seen him ever do that again, in the last four years. I feel cheated that he isn't who he promised to be, and that he hasn't done even a fraction of what he said he would do. I have put up with so much, supported him through so much, bailed him out so much and yet it's never good enough.

The smell of freedom is drifting upon the breeze around me

I can feel that the time is coming for him to go. The smell of freedom is drifting upon the breeze around me. I am scared, as we are so alone as a little family but then, if I allow him to stay, it will be just as bad. It could be worse. I know there will come that moment when I say 'enough'. But, when I say it their will no going back, which is why I know I have to be mentally strong and focused. I need to break the emotional ties.

I have given up trying to tell him how I am, or how I feel, as he always explodes and then punishes me for days on end. So I always say 'fine' if he asks if I'm OK. Yesterday, he asked and I said I was fine. He kept badgering me, as he could see I wasn't. I told him I was very lonely. I educate my daughter at home all week. I support her with an online school, so I never get a break or get to go out anywhere. The only thing my partner wants to do is work on his motorbike and go on holiday with his biker buddies. I finally cracked and told him the truth and, of course, he just started being nasty and sarcastic etc.

He never takes us anywhere, even for a walk or anything. I can't drive, so the only way I can get the kids out is to use cabs. I do this as much as I can, but, as we are at the doctors and the hospital a lot, I have to keep the cab fare money for that, mostly. He can drive, and we have a car, but he chooses not to take us out, ever. So, as I write this, Pat, I am being ignored and punished for having a voice. He hates me having a voice. I have told him all he wants is me to be a nodding doggy. Someone to pay the bills, wash his clothes and iron them, cook his food, buy him loads of stuff, never grumble, always have a ridiculous smile on my face and look nice. My partner is a professional man with a very good job, although he only contributes just for himself. He tells me that all the people he works with think he is amazing, wonderful, and charming. The best thing ever!

I care for my children round the clock, and we have crises every week that I have to sort out for them. Last year my son had two major operations. If I told you everything my kids have been through at the hands of adults and children in schools, as well as thinking about their own dad, you would be staggered. I have lost faith in human beings. This week, I discovered my son's cab driver and escort to his special school have been bullying him. He had been bending his fingers back, keeping his bags from him and calling him names. The school had noticed too and, as soon as I learnt how bad it was, I stopped the cabs and had a ding dong with LEA. My son internalised everything. He stopped eating and was so quiet. I had tried to find out what was going on, but all I could get from him were a few worries with school.

There were major issues with my daughter this week, too. But this is like most weeks. There is always something to deal with, whether it's their health, education or mental welfare. They are the most incredible people I have ever known, and I am so privileged to be their mummy. They make the sun come out for me each and every day. I know I am strong inside. When it's anything to do with the children, I am a lioness protecting her cubs at any expense. But, for myself, I am quite pathetic. I am getting stronger by the day and I know that slowly, very slowly I will get there.

Sorry Pat, I have waffled, but I thought I would send in some thoughts if they were of any help. Thank you for all of your support through your books and the site. It has helped me enormously. Kindest Regards Poppy.

     freedomprogramme@btinternet.com   www.freedomprogramme.co.uk

Chapter 7 – Tiger Lilly

Tiger Lilly

…I was married for 16 years to Clark. Our married life didn't start off very well. We lived in a very damp flat in rural Wales, money was always tight as Clark had purchased a sports car which was expensive to run and insure. Clark was also a heavy drinker and smoker. Even though we both worked (I was the higher earner, Clark frequently got the sack), our outgoings were always more than our incomings.

The condition of our flat was really bad. We had black mould, chronic condensation, everything was damp. I had no washing machine, phone or cooker. When I became pregnant with Becky, I really felt I had let my baby down living in such a horrible place. We quickly got into rent arrears because Clark spent so much money on his 'hobbies', which were fishing, cars, alcohol and, in hindsight, other women. I could never understand where our money went to, and every month was the same. Someone on a Freedom Programme recently said to me, about her life with an abuser, 'Same shit, different day'. That is exactly how my life was, and now I was pregnant for the first time.

I am, and was, a qualified early years practitioner, having trained as a nursery nurse. Before I met Clark, I had a very successful career working with young children and their families. I felt I had really let my baby down, and this led to severe depression which lasted throughout the pregnancy.

Clark would not talk about the baby, or what we could do about our living conditions. He would not attend antenatal classes. Because we were so short of money, I carried on working late into the pregnancy. This resulted in varicose veins and high blood pressure. I begged him to sell the car. The insurance, alone, was over £1,000 per year (this was 1989), but he refused saying I was selfish and the car was his only pleasure in life.

I ordered a pushchair and car seat from a colleague at work who had a catalogue. I could never keep up with the repayments and started to avoid her.

I knew people were talking about me, and this increased my anxiety and depression. I lied to work, saying I would be going back to my job so that I could receive maternity allowance after Becky was born. But, in reality, I knew that I was planning my escape back to Darlington (I didn't manage to escape until 2006), and I would never go back, because I owed money to my colleague and she had told all my workmates. I still wake up in a cold sweat some nights after having relived this episode in my dreams. My dad, eventually, sent her a cheque for the balance, but by the time I had 'confessed' to him, the damage was done.

I went off sick. I did not get a 'baby shower' or cards or anything for my baby, as I had seen other pregnant colleagues get, because everyone thought I was a thief and a liar. I was completely ostracised and did not have one friend when I was pregnant with my first child.

I was in a desperate situation. Clark spent days and nights away from me, saying he couldn't get home after the pub; he'd had too much to drink and couldn't drive so he'd stayed at a friends. I was terrified I would go in to labour and he wouldn't be there. We were not on the phone and it was in the days before mobiles. A month before Becky was born I persuaded Clark that we should move in with his parents. He readily agreed, partly because we could do a 'moonlight' flit due to rent arrears and partly because he was a 'mummy's boy'. His parents were also heavy drinkers and smokers.

When we moved in with his parents, he told them that I was mentally ill and needed looking after whilst he was at work. They then treated me as if I had the plague and they would catch it. Because of their drinking and smoking I spent all the time in my bedroom.

I often thought about suicide, but I would feel Becky kicking inside me and could not bring myself to do it. Clark told me that the sight of my huge stomach disgusted him and he would spend the evenings drinking and smoking with his parents in the living room and then sleep on the sofa. I was completely alone and too ashamed to tell my family, who were in Darlington, about the way I was living. I thought I had made my bed and now I had to lie in it.

My provisions for Becky amounted to a pack of three white romper suits, a stolen pushchair and car seat, a second hand baby bath and a pack of bibs. I had no money for nappies or maternity bras or clothes.

Becky was born after 18 hours labour. Clark had to be dragged in to see the birth by some very irate midwives. By the end of the 18 hours labour they had become thoroughly pissed off with him because, instead of being a loving and attentive husband, rubbing my back and telling me to breathe, he had been found asleep in a bed on the ward, intoxicated and abusive.

As soon as Becky was born, he went off to wet the baby's head. I did not see him for three days. During our stay in hospital I had to borrow sanitary towels and nappies from another mum on the ward. Luckily for Becky I had chosen to breastfeed, otherwise I think she may have starved. Clark then arrived with his mum to take me home. We had to stop at Tesco on the way back to get some beers in, and he made a fuss when I bought some nappies. He said, 'She (meaning three day old Becky) had better not be using all my beer money, or there will be trouble'.
His mum laughed.

And trouble there was. Within days of arriving home from hospital Clark began physically abusing me. This physical abuse lasted until I left him in 2006. Becky was born in 1991. Clark resented Becky from the moment she was born. When he saw me breastfeeding her he would call her a 'leech' or a 'tick'.

Yet, in front of the few friends we had, he would sing my praises and walk around holding Becky as if he were a doting dad. It was a very confusing time, and whenever I tried to talk to him about things he would say I was 'mad' or 'mental', that I was a 'kill joy' and just talked about babies all the time. I really thought I was going mad.

Things came to a head when a health visitor did a home visit and saw how I was living - stuck in one room in a cramped house with horrible in-laws. She asked me if I was suffering from domestic violence. I said 'No'. That night, I managed to ring my dad in Darlington when everyone had gone to the pub. He had recently visited me with my sister and was visibly shocked at the state I was in. He'd had words with Clark then, but all that happened was that I got the cold shoulder from Clark and his parents and more abuse about Becky.

When my dad answered the phone all I could say was 'dad'. All my dad could say was, 'I'll come and get you in the morning. Be ready at eight'. The next day, I left Wales and went home with my six-week-old daughter. My dad took me straight to the GP, and I was diagnosed with mastitis (I couldn't afford a maternity bra) and severe PND.

Then the phone calls started; the persuading, the head working, relentless pressure and coercion. This resulted in Clark joining me in Darlington, promising he would change, he loved us etc etc. We then lived in a council house for the next two years, and then we bought my family home, which was the house that I had grown up in, from my dad and we stayed in Darlington until 2004.

I had two more children with Clark. Clare was born in 1993, and Michael was born in 2002. Michael was conceived through rape by Clark, my husband. He was also born nine weeks early. I suffered a bleeding in the lining of the brain and Michael was born by emergency caesarean with breathing problems. Clark abandoned us in hospital and did not tell my family that both Michael and I were nearly dying. Luckily, one of the midwives was a friend of my sister, and told her that I was in hospital fighting for my life with no-one there.

I didn't see Michael for five days because I was in and out of consciousness. When I eventually got down to the SCBU to see him, on his medical notes were the words 'dad disappeared, mum has made no contact'. When I saw those words I fainted from grief. Michael weighed 2lbs 4oz. He was fighting to breathe and I hadn't even been there for him, and I didn't know where his dad was.

Because of this, our aftercare from the health visitor was more intensive than for the two previous pregnancies. Clark resented the frequent visits from the health visitor to our home. He would be openly hostile to her if he was around (he worked shifts). He would not let me attend appointments to hospital for MRI scans. He would take the buggy in the car to work. The health visitor asked me if I was suffering from domestic violence. I said 'No'.

When Michael came home from the special care baby unit weighing 3 pounds, Clark punched me in the arm whilst I was holding him, just missing his tiny head. When Michael was one, Clark began a sexual relationship with a woman from his work. Afterwards, I was told that this poor lady went from man to man and was known as the 'factory bike'. Clark had unprotected sex with her. I had to go for tests for sexual diseases.

It took me five years to leave Clark because he always kept Clare with him. I just could not leave her behind. Clare has more emotional problems than Becky or Michael because she was Clark's favourite. He was openly full of contempt and rage concerning Becky and Michael. He called Michael a 'sissy boy' or 'mummy's boy' (he was just three years old when I escaped).

He said Becky 'hated him', and so he would hate her, and it was her own fault. Becky was 14 when I left.

The girls were very bright and high achievers throughout their school lives.

This was a miracle, really, as their home life was nothing short of a nightmare. There was always a tense atmosphere. We were always in debt and frequently had bailiffs at the door. The phone was cut off on many an occasion. I couldn't regularly provide healthy meals for them. We never had a holiday. The police were often at our home, either because Clark was fighting in town at weekends, or because the neighbours had heard us fighting. Clark regularly got the sack, and this contributed to our chronic debt. This has affected my credit rating to this day.

When Becky was six and Clare was four, I got a job at their school as a teaching assistant. One day, Becky got told off by her teacher for writing the same things for 'news' in her writing book week in week out.

Poor Becky, she could hardly write the truth:

> "On Saturday, daddy pulled mummy's hair and pushed her on the floor. When she tried to get up, daddy hit her with a chair. Mummy was worried because my little sister was in the bath and she might drown. Daddy told mummy to stay on the floor until he told her to get up.

> "On Sunday, I watched CBeebies with my fingers in my ears because I didn't want to hear the shouting. I looked after my little sister because mummy was crying all day because we haven't got any money. We had peanut butter sandwiches for dinner and water out of the tap."

Instead, every time Becky had to write about her 'news' she wrote:

"On Saturday we went to the park. On Sunday I played with Clare with Barbies."

Clark frequently stormed into my workplace demanding money or making a scene of some sort. This was so embarrassing and really bad for my career. I had to tell so many lies, I couldn't go out with colleagues socially, and people avoided me because Clark's behaviour was so bad. He embarrassed me at parents' evenings, school shows, it was just a nightmare.

This culminated in the head teacher asking me to escort Clark off the premises on one occasion, as he had arrived at school with a hammer threatening to bash another dad's brains in who he thought was 'after' me.

This was the place where my daughters received their education. It should have been a time where they felt happy and had lots of friends. Instead, they never went to other children's birthday parties and they had to tell so many lies to cover up what was actually going on at the weekends.

As I mentioned previously, Clark began to see someone else around this time. Michael was still a baby. I was recovering from a traumatic birth and working part-time. I found out about Lorna as Clark used Becky's mobile phone to send sex texts. The upset this caused Becky was immense. She was 12 at the time. I don't know how many of these texts she saw, but I will never forget the day when she handed me her mobile phone, burst into tears and ran off. The text was about anal sex.

Lorna finished with Clark. I was then left with a husband who expected me to comfort him because his girlfriend had packed him in. I was so exhausted and ill that when he suggested that we sell up and move to a lovely village in Wales, I just let things happen. It was like I was in a bad dream. I watched as my family home was sold and everything that I loved just fell apart.

63

 freedomprogramme@btinternet.com   www.freedomprogramme.co.uk

Very conveniently, Clark managed to fall out with my entire family and my dad around this time. So when my house was sold, after three days on the market, and everything went into storage, no-one waved us off or wished us well. No-one planned to visit us as soon as we were settled.

The girls were wrenched from their schools and friends, their granddad wasn't around anymore. They were dumped in a Welsh speaking school, with an abusive father and a depressed, ill mother and little baby.

Clark was in his element. We rented an enormous house by the sea (I daily wanted to drown myself in it). He had £120,000 in the bank from the sale of our house. He was king of the castle and lorded it over everyone. He soon started to make enemies in the village because he would be arrogant, rude and chat up their girlfriends and wives. I have never felt as lonely as when I've sat next to Clark in the local pub, surrounded by people. They hated him. One lady asked me why I stayed with 'that bastard'. I couldn't answer.

Michael started to have frequent bronchiolitis around this time due to being a premature baby. He was diagnosed with asthma and he developed phobias around meal times. Mealtimes were so stressful in our home.

Becky was so depressed. She really missed her granddad and her friends. She couldn't speak to me because I was crying all the time. If I wasn't crying I was hiding from the neighbours. She looked after Michael when she wasn't at school. Clark kept Clare with him at all times. When she wasn't at school, she was with him at work (he was self employed doing property maintenance then), or in the local pub. She would often be there until two in the morning at weekends. She was 11.

One night, I went out with some girls from the village for a meal. I got really drunk and told them all about my life, well some of it. The next day, I had a near breakdown when I remembered what I'd said and to whom. I shook for days and was so scared. It was then I really began to think about the possibility of escaping. I thought, 'If I stay, he will kill me'.

I confided in Becky and she began to collect some of Michael's toy cars in a bag. Every morning she would look at me and I would shake my head slightly. She always looked crushed when I did this, and I knew I couldn't stay much longer. I was desperate and frightened.

January 6th 2006

New Years Eve had been especially grim. Michael was ill and I was nursing him. Clark told me he was going to the pub and would be back to see the New Year in with me, and I was to stay up. I fell asleep next to Michael as I had been watching his breathing. The next thing I knew I was being dragged down the stairs by my hair to celebrate the New Year. This time Clark hit me in the face, something he had never done before. He had always hit me on my body, legs and arms (I never wore short sleeves).

On the morning of January 6th I woke up with a strong conviction that I was to leave him that day. I got together the kids' favourite cuddly toys, my passport and £120 of child benefit that I had hidden in a Tampax box. I got on a train in the village, and changed trains at Birmingham for Darlington. When we got to Birmingham I told the children that we weren't going back to Wales. Michael cried so much for his transformer toys. Becky went pale and put her arms round me. She was really scared. Clare shouted 'NO!' and repeatedly thumped me in the leg.

I was amazed that I still had money in my purse! I was determined that this was it. I was quite firm with them all. I didn't shout. I think they were relieved I was taking charge. With all of this money (honestly I'd never had so much money to myself) I took them for a MacDonald's (that diffused the

situation) and then got the train to my sister's
house in Darlington.

Separation was a very dangerous time for us. I honestly thought
that Clark would find me and kill me. After I escaped from
Wales to Darlington, he left a message on my mobile which said,
'When I find you I'm going to burn you alive and you'll never
see the children alive again'.

We left my sisters after he had found us and had dragged me into
the street by my hair. She had to call the police. She told
me that I couldn't live there as her 11-year-old daughter had
witnessed the incident. She was angry with me. She has not
spoken to me since.

From there, we sofa surfed at friends houses. Clark always found
us. My nephew was a builder. He told me I could stay in
a house he was renovating. The house was gutted. There were
wires hanging down. There was no hot water, just concrete
floors, no flooring or carpets. He had not put all the windows
in. It was January. Compared to life with Clark it was heaven!

One day I was spotted going to the launderette with a buggy full
of clothes by an ex-boyfriend who was an architect. He could not
believe what he was seeing. Last time he had seen me I was a
gorgeous blonde-haired blue-eyed successful career woman with
everything to live for.

We lived in this building for about six weeks until Clark found
us again. This time the police were called by some people who
heard us screaming. The police took us to a refuge.

We were re-housed in the summer of 2006. Then Clark
continued his abuse through the courts. In 2008 I represented
myself in court. I was not eligible for Legal Aid as I had resumed
my studies on a degree course, and so did not qualify, and I
could not afford a solicitor. I secured a court order that Clark

should have supervised contact with Michael every other week. He wanted unsupervised contact every weekend.

Six weeks after I had left him he had become engaged to Paula, a teacher. Paula joined Clark in his continued abuse through the court system, saying she had evidence that I was mentally unstable and not fit to take care of my children. Paula had a lot of credibility and I had a fight on my hands with CAFCASS. They kept on saying, 'Paula is a teacher. She knows what she is on about'.

CAFCASS kept on asking me for evidence that I had been abused. They said Clark had rights, and that the children needed to get to know Paula, as she would be a part of their lives. I was portrayed as being uncooperative and emotionally unstable.

The CAFCASS officer said I was bitter and jealous about Paula, and that I should 'move on' with my life. The children were interviewed. I had six home visits. I was accused of brainwashing the children because they had said in their interviews that they would not see their dad.

I had to prove I was not mentally ill by taking psychiatric assessments and tests. Clark and Paula did not even have a home visit. Once the court order was in place, they had contact with Michael three times, and then they literally 'disappeared'. My children have not seen Clark since 2008.

Last year, I learnt from the CSA that they have had a baby together. I pray for that baby. I have never received any monies for the provision of the children. There is no-one who will make Clark accountable, as he says he is self employed.

To date: Becky

Becky is now 20. She still lives at home. She has a full-time job at Zara. She is going to Venice with her friend, Veronica, in two weeks time. She has paid for it herself, sorted out insurance, hotels, transport, everything independently. She adores Michael. They are very close.

He is the trendiest ten-year-old you will ever see, dressed entirely in Zara clothes for boys. Becky and Michael are going on a cruise together next year around the Mediterranean. Becky is paying for it. She wants Michael to travel. She loves fashion. She looks like Audrey Hepburn. She got thirteen GCSEs and four A-Levels, including an A* for English and history.

Becky tried to go to Uni, but came home after a term. Her dad had been in contact with her via Facebook and went through the whole process of rejecting her again. This time he did it online. The stress caused Becky to have a stomach ulcer at the age of 18. She doesn't have a boyfriend. She says boys her age are 'players', out for what they can get and to mess with your mind. She found it hard when I married Paul in 2009. She is now warming to him as he has been wise to always be consistent and to keep his promises to her. He doesn't try to be her dad, but he tries to be her 'Paul' instead. She suffers from depression. She gets over anxious about money. She gets homesick easily.

Clare

Clare is 18. She is very artistic and creative, with an amazing sense of humour. She is really pretty and always looks stunning. She loves her boyfriend, Seb, who is a musician in a band. She takes photos of the band for their promos. She loves music and animals. She also got thirteen GCSEs. She was really popular at school, and had loads of friends. She has done charity work in Spain and Poland. She gets on well with Paul. She calls him 'Perfect Paul'. She is brilliant at cooking. She loves having

people over for dinner and then playing board games. She has invented a new twist on the board game 'Guess who?' Instead of saying, 'Has the person got a ginger moustache?' you ask, 'Is the person a social worker' or, 'Is the person running for president of the USA?' It's hilarious after a couple of glasses
of red. Try it.

Clare loved Clark and was his favourite. Clare finds having a relationship with Becky and Michael difficult. She wants to move in with her boyfriend, but can't afford it. There have been arguments between all of us, because Clare says she hates being at home with us because she is the odd one out. She depends on Seb to make her happy. Seb frequently finishes with her, because he can't cope with this pressure to make her happy all the time. When he asks for time out she becomes hysterical. They separated three weeks ago. She has hit Seb on occasion. Clare did not take her A-Level exams. She has been referred for counselling by our GP. She has depression and acute anxiety. She just can't handle rejection. She doesn't know what she wants to do with her life. She has started seeing Seb again.
Now she is at his house all the time. She won't answer
her phone.

Michael

I wish you could meet Michael. He would have you in stitches in seconds. He is really clever and can tell you how nuclear power works. He plays the clarinet. His recent certificate from school reads: 'for an excellent attitude and for taking people just as they are and never judging'. He loves to go out for meals and holidays. He loved going to New York after Paul and I were just married. It was the children's first time on an aeroplane. I don't think he will ever forget it. He loves animals and meeting new people.

He doesn't remember Clark. He remembers the refuge because he always won the kids bingo. He loves Paul. Paul is an engineer, a Star Wars geek and can build Lego. They are best mates, always having water fights and putting fake spiders on the stairs. He loves to wear his life-size Cyberman helmet whilst doing his homework. He puts Post-it notes on his remote control tarantula which say, 'get up now I want breakfast'. We are often woken up by a giant tarantula coming into our bedroom bearing messages of this kind.

Michael still has a tendency to be a fussy eater, but we ignore it. He hates giving anything away or giving toys to charity shops, even his clothes which don't fit him anymore. I always have to build up to these times with lots of reassurances and reasoning. I don't think he has ever got over the shock of losing all of his toys, his pets and his home.

I once asked a Professor on my degree course (in early childhood studies) the question: 'What do neglected or abused children remember?' He replied: 'They remember what they didn't have. Love, warmth, security, safety, food, shelter, happy parents, clean clothes, things that everyone needs to make their lives work.'

I think that Michael doesn't remember the abuse, but he remembers the loss, the shock, the fear. However, Michael is the least affected of the three, the happiest, the most confident, the most empathetic and the most trusting.

I think that says it all.

Me

I am now 48. In 2010 I stopped looking over my shoulder every time I left the house. I am studying to be a barrister in family law, specialising in domestic abuse and child contact issues. I am a Freedom Programme facilitator, having run four over the last year. I am married to the 'Perfect Paul' and we are doing life together, working it out as we go along. Paul is incredibly biased and says I am the most amazing woman he has ever known.

I don't feel amazing much of the time. I battle with my weight and depression. I struggle with friendships. I'm not quite sure what to do with a friend once I've got one. I've been taken advantage of by needy people. I'm just learning about boundaries. I remembered that I used to like knitting, so have taken that up again. I find it hard to cry. I can't listen to music unless it's Classic FM, which is something that I'm not really into. I don't have much in common with other women. If I don't make a conscious effort to be sociable I can be withdrawn and isolate myself. I still have a feeling that I've got something to hide.

I miss my photos of the children, but if I close my eyes I can remember what they looked like. I feel like a failure as a mother half the time, but what I do say to myself when I doubt my parenting is, "Think of the alternative. You could still be with HIM!' Then I am absolutely convinced, without a shadow of a doubt that, by leaving Clark, the children are in a better place despite their issues. Because, quite honestly, who hasn't got issues?

Chapter 8 – Lilly of the Valley

Dad was a wagon driver and mum was a nurse, and I had one sister. I was always a daddy's girl, and I only really found out in the last 10 years that he was a perpetrator of domestic violence against my mother. I remember hearing screaming when I was young, and having to hold my sister and tell her it was okay, but I never really knew what was happening, I just knew that I had to look after my sister.

I can't tell you how long that went on for. I can't remember, but I know that it really affected me in a very scary way. When I got older, I think I blocked it out and couldn't remember anything for a long time until I started to get flashbacks when I was about 14, only they weren't visual, it was sound. I will sound like a lunatic saying this, but it used to start with a whistle in my ear, and then it sounded like I was in a tunnel, but then the shouting would start and it would grow louder and louder until it was just a scream, and physically it would feel like my movements would get faster and faster. I use to cry and beg the voices to stop, but they never would. This went on for a number of years, and people thought I was crazy at times. I even thought that I was mentally ill. I was too scared to tell anyone in case they said that I was. I don't know why they stopped, they just did. I can't remember the last time that it happened.

After my parents separated, when I was 10, my childhood was full of moving and having to start again. I was passed about like an inanimate object between my parents. I felt like I was just a pawn in their own game of revenge: "Let's see who can hurt each other the most, stuff our daughter!" That's what it felt like. The worst move came just after my 15th birthday. I hadn't seen my mum for a long time, and at that moment I really didn't want to, but my dad's new wife thought that I should have my mum in my life, so she set up a meeting. We had dinner together, along with dad's wife. At the end, mum said that she would ring me

72

and arrange another day. She rang me the day after and arranged to meet me for coffee the next day.

My dad also wanted to speak to my mum when I had finished, and I was then told to go to my room.

The next day, at coffee with my mum, she asked me if I knew what my dad had said. I didn't so she told me. "Your dad said that there is no room for you anymore, so you have to come and live with me, or you are going into care." To say that I was shocked is an understatement, but worse was yet to come. When I got home and went up to my room, I found my room already packed up, and outside the house was a removal van. All my things were put in the van, including me! And yet no one said a word to me. I didn't see my dad again until about 4 years later.

This was the norm for me, I'd spend a few years with my mum, and that meant that I wasn't allowed any contact with my dad, or that side of the family. Then I would spend a few years with dad, and I couldn't see my mum or my sisters. I must say, the person who made all these rules was my mum, and not my dad.

By the time I was 10 years old, I had been sexually abused twice. The first time I was three. The abusers were the babysitter and her friend, with the use of a bicycle pump. This was performed on both me and my sister, who was two at the time. The second when I was nine years old, and I have to say that it was this abuse that dominated my life for a long time. The man was, at the time, about to become my step-grandfather. He was 70. For about six months, my sister and I were sent down to his house every night, so that my mother could sit and talk in peace about the separation with my dad, and the custody battle over me.

The visits seemed okay, at first, but then it started to get uncomfortable for me. He would send my sister out of the room for silly things and then start talking to me, saying dirty things that he wanted to do and see. As every night progressed, more

73

and more things happened and he began his barrage of sexual abuse on me. I remember him sending my sister out of the room one night and I saw her looking from the crack in the door until he was finished with me. Then she came back in and said that she could not find what he had sent her for.

I never told anyone about the abuse. The only comment I ever made was to my sister, and all I said was that I hated going because he does things to me. She never said anything either. It was a long time before I ever spoke of it again. I was so scared that no-one would believe me. Who would believe a nine-year-old over a 70-year-old man? Even if they did, would they say that I had deserved it, and it was my fault? I remember mum telling me once that I dressed like a hooker. So maybe it was my fault.

For years I struggled with what had happened, not talking to anyone. One day, when I had gone to live with my dad, I saw the old man and couldn't cope with feelings that I felt, and the way he smiled at me gave me nightmares. I wrote a letter to a problem page, but in the end I never sent it off. I was too scared that someone might recognise me from my writing, so I hid it under my bed, and forgot all about it, until my dad found it.

I had gone to visit my mum, and my dad picked me up to take me home. He told me that he had found the letter and he wanted to know what it was about and was it true. I just burst out crying and couldn't control myself. I was 14 and I had held on to it for five years. Just then, in that moment, five years' worth of tears just flooded out of me. Firstly, I think out of sheer relief that I could talk about it to someone and, second, out of fear of what was going to happen to me now.

Dad called the police and it was going to court. There was evidence in the form of medical reports from when I was nine. They stated that my hymen had been broken and that something had happened to me. I'd been getting infections down below and people thought it strange that, at nine years old, I was getting these infections. But, because I wouldn't tell anyone what had happened to me, my mother had accused my father in court of sexually abusing me. In that moment, my father's relationship with me was destroyed. We couldn't even give each other a hug anymore. Try and imagine, for one moment, how it felt, sitting in front of my dad, telling him about the abuse, knowing that he couldn't put his arms around me, because I didn't speak out when I should have done.

It was the 90s when all this happened and, at that time, in child abuse cases you had to have witness statements to prove it. Luckily for me I had my sister. The police came to see me to tell me that they were going to go and see her and my mum that day to gather statements from them, and that they would call back and see me after to let me know how it had gone. When they came back, I could tell by their expressions on their faces that the news wasn't good, but I don't think I was expecting what I got.

My sister had told the police that nothing had happened and that I was lying, and my mum gave a glowing character reference for my abuser, finishing with the comment that he would never had hurt any of us, and why would he hurt me and not my sister? Without the witness statements it was thrown out of court for lack of evidence, and he then went on to hurt another little girl, and I was engulfed with guilt for that as well. I was called a liar. I'm sad to say that that situation is still the same today. I asked my sister once, when we were alone, why she had done that, and she replied that it was my punishment for leaving mum and going to live with Dad. I told mum, but she wouldn't believe me. The pain I suffered from what my mum and sister did to me was more intense than the abuse, and the damage it caused was so immense, I don't think that I will ever recover from that.

I lost all control of everything, I felt worthless, ugly, and I thought that my purpose in life was to be used and abused.

I started using drugs, cannabis at first, as we all do, but then I went on to gas, pills, LSD and speed, I went very far down the line in a very quick space of time. I started to sleep around, longing to be touched in a nice way, but it never really happened. I was desperate to be loved but I soon came to realise that love didn't exist. Pain, violence, destruction, misery were real, and I felt them on a daily basis. I had sex for money or drugs, and sometimes just for a bed to sleep in. I didn't care about me. Why should I? No one else did.

By the time I was 18, I was on the street and homeless. I was a mess. I was given a room in a hostel in Burnley. It wasn't perfect, but at least it was a roof over my head. I remember sitting there in my empty room, thinking about my life and how I had ended up there. I didn't have a clue that it stemmed back to the violence in the home when I was a kid, and that I now believed that is normal life. No. I just thought that I must have been a bad person from day one, and that I did deserve all that had happened to me. But I also knew I didn't want this life and that I wanted to do something about it.

With the help of the hostel staff I got myself clean and off the drugs, I won't pretend that it was easy because, it wasn't, but I did it. 15 years, now, I have been clean. Then I met Mike.
I thought that he was fantastic, and I loved being with him. He was in the hostel because he had just come out of prison, and he said that he wanted a better life. So did I, which made it a perfect match.

Mike stripped me of all my belongings and my new-found confidence. He assaulted me and imprisoned me for years.
I couldn't complain, because, when I did, he became violent with me. He would repeatedly hit me. I would scream for help, hoping that a neighbour would hear me, and come and help me, but no one came. You hear people making comments, as to why we don't just leave at the first punch, but let me tell you,

I stayed as long as I did out of fear of what he would do if I left him, and I was right.

The night I ended it he tried to kill me. He threw me all over the house, then he wrapped his hands round my throat and squeezed as tight as he could. I can't tell you how I felt in at that moment. I can tell you about the look of hate in his eyes, and I could see that he wanted me dead. I really believed that I was going to die. I remember that feeling of my chest going tighter and feeling like someone had put an anvil on my chest. I must have passed out, because when I came to he was gone. That was the first time I ever called the police.

I was a mess with handprints round my neck. I will never forget what the officer said to me, "Yeah well you've no broken bones". Months later, it went to court. The charge was common assault. He got two years probation, to run concurrently with what he was already doing, and a £75 compensation order.
Of course, I never received any of that. He was also charged with a car theft that day, and got a fine of £200 for that.
The car was worth more than I was in the eyes of the law.

By the time all this had happened, I had a full time job and a house of my own, but I couldn't cope with that smack in the face off the justice system. The situation was made even worse because he kept coming round to my house. Every time I rang the police they just said, "Unless he actually says the words that he is going to kill you, then there is nothing that we can do". Thanks for that.

As a result, I once again became depressed and on medication. I couldn't deal with work and lost my job, which meant that I was now in debt and was going to lose my home. I decided that I just needed to get away from all it. That's when I moved to Spain.

The plan was to sing out there, and to find somewhere to live. It took a while, but I did it eventually. I got a job as a cook in a

77

cafe during the day, and managed to get some booking for shows at night, as well as finding an apartment. Then I met David, the next abuser.

Life was not good. I would cook, clean and be there for sex on demand. I was called every name under the sun. We got a dog in the hope that I would have some company, and be able to go for walks during the day whilst he was in bed, but he would beat the dog. He became so jealous of the dog around me that he even built a barrier across the whole apartment, so that the dog couldn't go near me. I couldn't take the dog out for a walk, so he would wee in the apartment and then get battered for it, and I would get told that it was my fault because I didn't take him out. The neighbours used to hear him beating the dog and would make comments at me and stare at me in the street, like it was me who was doing it.

I had decided that I needed a break away to sort my head out and to make some money, because we had nothing, all the wages went on drugs for him. My dad came and got me, and I went to stay with him. On this visit my dad attacked me twice, and split my head open. My mum cared for me after the attack. In that moment, I had lost who I was. I had always been a daddy's girl, and loved him so much that I had never believed my mum when she told me what he had done to her. I had hated her for it. Yet, here I was, in her home, being cared for. She said, "Of all the things that I thought he would do, I never thought that he would hurt you."

If I said that I had lost the plot before, I don't know what you would call what was happening to me now. But it would still take another year or so before the outcome would be seen.

I went back to Spain, and to David, thinking that life had been better there. The situation with him worsened. I was going mad. I was hearing the voices again, and the amount of times I tried to kill myself had gone beyond a joke. I had tried lots of times before, when I was younger, but now I really wanted to die. Just when things couldn't get any worse for me, I found out that I was pregnant. I returned to the UK, and David insisted on coming with me.

I just wanted to be home with my mum. I knew she would be waiting for me when we arrived. As soon as I saw her, I ran over to her and burst out crying and just held her. I just wanted to burst out and tell her everything, but I couldn't. We found a flat, just down the road from my mum's, and I felt that at least I had some support around me.

The abuse was unbearable, and he never stopped. I was working from home because we still never had any money, even though he was working, he would give me a pittance to try and run the place on, so I had no choice. When he came back home from work, I would get the same response. "You fat fucking slag, what have you been doing all day, the house is a shit tip, stupid whore". Every day was the same. He would sing at me "SLAG" and then laugh when I started to cry.

He would come right over to my face and spit at me as he told me how ugly and fat I was.

After my daughter was born, his attacks on me got worse. One day, something snapped, I had just got out of the bath with my little girl, throughout the whole day he was on me, never stopping. I calmly wrapped my daughter in her towel and walked into the front room and placed her down on the couch. I stood up, collapsed her swing, which was a big metal frame, and swung at him, again, and again, and again but he just laughed louder and louder. I dragged him into the hallway by his hair and wrapped the Hoover cord round his neck and pulled. I wanted him to die, I wanted it to stop, all I could think was, 'If he wasn't here we would be OK'. I could hear him choking, but then I heard my baby cry out, and I looked down at my hands and let go. I stood back and just looked at him on the floor. I thought I had done it, I thought I had killed him, but then he moved and groaned. I ran and got my daughter and locked myself in the bedroom.

That was my Turning Point. I knew that I had become what had been done to me, and I knew that if I didn't do something about it now, I would lose my little girl and I wasn't about to let that happen. I left him when my daughter was 10 months old. I got a house from the council. I went to see my doctor and told him that I needed help. I got help from the Women's Centre, and also had a family support worker. It took me a long time, but I did it. I started volunteering and went back to college. He never left me alone, but it didn't matter, because I had won and I was free. He still plagues my life. He plays the loving father now, and buys her affection, he does his best to make things difficult for me, but I don't care.

You would have thought that I would have learned my lesson, but you would be wrong. I stayed on my own for a long time, but four years ago I met the man who is now my husband. At the start of the relationship I thought he was wonderful, and he did everything for me. The problem came from the fact that he was a recovering addict, and he had HEP C strand 1 A. This is the worst kind and he was about to start his treatment for it. He had already decided that he wanted to marry me, and I stupidly allowed myself to be whisked off my feet. The plans were in place and a date set. Then his treatment started. I knew it wasn't going to be nice, but I didn't expect what I got.

He slept most of the time. That was fine. I could handle a sleepy man, but when he wasn't asleep all hell would break loose. I remember having an argument with him, and going out for a walk to cool off. When I came back, he pinned me up against the wall with a knife to my throat and asked me who was coming to get him. He smashed the house to bits, doors, walls, stereo, Freeview and mobile phones. I didn't know what to do. I spoke to the GP, the hospital, the nurse and they all told me the same thing. This is one of the unfortunate side effects of the Interferon treatment. Men become aggressive and violent at times, and women become suicidal.

I couldn't believe it. After everything I had been through, here I was again, only this time the medical services were telling me that it was the medication. I made a decision that I would support him through this but, if it continued after the treatment had finished, he would be gone. In a way, I feel like I deserved what I got after that. He pushed me, slapped me, punched me, and smothered me with a pillow, but once the medication stopped the violence stopped.

Something else started instead, he relapsed on drugs, which has devastated our marriage. He has taken every penny off me and run me into the ground. I'm in debt that I'm struggling to correct. I am on my own again with my daughter. She is seven and she is wonderful. She, too, has come through so much, and has come through the other side. She loves my husband and prays every night that he will get better and come home.

Meanwhile, things are moving forwards for us. I have a great job (my dream job I might add). Through that, I have read the book 'Living with the Dominator' and attended the three day Freedom Programme professional training. When we did the session on the 'Effects of Abuse on Children' on the last day, it broke my heart. Although I realised that my dad did beat my mum a while back, I never realised the impact that it had on me and my life. It took me a long time to escape the abuse, and I don't even think that I have escaped fully just yet.

So that's the shortened version of my life. A lot is missing, but I couldn't fit everything in, and there really wasn't time. I hope it helps. There is always life after abuse…

Chapter 9 – Freesia

I am a man. Freesias were my grandmother's favourite flowers. The first six years of my life were wonderful. I lived with my parents and grandparents. Everyone worked hard, and we had a good standard of living. I was sent to school in nice clothes, we had good quality food and the house was clean and comfortable. I do not remember my parents ever showing me any physical affection, but my grandparents adored me and I loved them both dearly. Granddad read to me and taught me to count, to write and to read. When he read to me, he did wonderful things like enacting characters from the story. I remember him wearing a sheet as a cloak, with a colander on his head as a helmet and brandishing a broom handle as a sword.

I was sent to a Catholic infant's school where the nuns enforced strict rules, and they taught the children to behave properly, and to know wrong from right. I did very well, and my reports were glowing. I was a teacher's pet.

My little, safe, happy world came to an end when I was six. Grandma died and Granddad went to live with my uncle and aunt. He gave my parents the house, but everything started to unravel. Looking back, I now realise that both my parents were people who would now be described as underachievers.
They had been able to function as parents solely because my grandparents were in charge. They had been the adults. Without them my parents were lost. I see now that my mother was particularly vulnerable.

My mother was preyed upon by Stan, a very abusive married man who impregnated her with my half sister. My father's reaction was to subject my mother and myself to extreme physical violence. I remember him picking mum up and throwing her across the room. She smashed in to the wall and slid down to the floor. Part of one of my fingers are still missing from the time he slammed a door on my hand.

His reign of terror ended when he stormed out of the house and we phoned Granddad who came round and changed the locks. At first it was wonderful to be on my own with mum, but this did not last.

The next ten years were dreadful. Stan took over our lives. He remained with his wife, but also ruled our household. He attacked me physically, and he destroyed my mother emotionally. She was completely controlled by him. When she was pregnant he insisted that we spent all day every day at his mother's house, instead of in our own home. Our house became dirty and neglected. I remember persuading mum to stay in our house, to clean it and do the washing. We had a lovely day, doing the housework together. We worked hard, and eventually everywhere was clean and tidy. When he found out that we had not spent the day with his mother, Stan had a huge tantrum and we did not dare to do this again.

Stan persuaded mum to sell our house, and he kept the money. He refused to let her work, and promised, for years, that he was just about to leave his wife. This situation lasted for the next twenty years until he died. Mum became a wreck. She was drinking and chain smoking, and we had no money for food. One night, she was so deranged that she tried to smother me with a pillow. We moved from one horrible flat to another, often without electricity.

I was sent to several different schools in scruffy dirty clothes. I had no friends, and I was bullied. My half sister and I were virtually starving most of the time. Amazingly, I behaved well and tried hard at school. When I look back I think I was saved by the memory of my early years with my grandparents. I remembered the lessons I learned from them, and from the nuns. Consequentially, I was able to observe my own miserable home life and know that things could be different.

In spite of everything, I did so well at school that I had the opportunity to go to university to study medicine. Stan forced me to leave school and take a job which I hated because he wanted my wages. Eventually, I broke away from the situation at home and made a life for myself. I have always rejected the behaviour and attitudes of men like Stan and my father. I respect women and enjoy their company. I have been happily married to the same woman for twenty six years.

I am writing this for Pat's book because I suffered at the hands of these men, and I would love to protect other children from being abused like this. I want everyone who reads this to remember that children have no voice. They have no power.
If their mother does not protect them, nobody else will.

Chapter 10 The Freedom Programme

Magnolia

..Michael's reign continued with my children for another three years through contact orders etc. The Freedom Programme came into my life in 2006. I trained as a facilitator in 2009, and I have run a Freedom Programme in my area, with the help of other facilitators, for the last two years. The Freedom Programme started a change in our lives. Initially, it helped me to minimise the effect he was having on us day-by-day. I was able to counter his abuse and began quietly teaching my children non-abusive behaviours that flew in the face of Michael's Dominator beliefs.

The journey back from domestic abuse for my children and I has been a long and challenging one, but without The Freedom Programme, where would we be now?! It doesn't bear thinking about.

I now see that the effects of domestic abuse didn't end when the relationship did. There was a halt in the immediate abuse, and the effects got less and less as his stranglehold on my family was released. I am now free to be the mum I want to be to my children, without him sabotaging every aspect of our lives. My girls are free of Michael, for now. His interest waned when his attempts to upset me were met with a poker face, and when he finally saw that he had no control over my life. Although he was, virtually, given permission by the court to continue to abuse my children and me, he didn't get a single clue out of me that his abuse was having an effect. The Freedom Programme gave me strength to counteract his poison.

Peter attended a men's programme with Pat, and showed his growing wisdom in front of lots of dominating men. He knew that Michael's abuse was about controlling and upsetting me. Peter is now 14, a believer in sexual equality and a respecter of women. The girls in his group of friends all tell me, "He's the best brought up boy out of all the boys in our group", "He treats girls with respect", "We wish all of the boys were like Peter".

Have we recovered? Have we overcome the poisonous effects of domestic abuse? Most definitely! My son Peter is testament to the fact that we have made it. Because of The Freedom Programme, Peter and I know, and appreciate, the quality of our lives now...

Daisy

Life with my children after leaving the Dominator

...In the first couple of months after leaving my three-year-old had to comfort me so much. I feel really ashamed that I let her see me that way, but I just couldn't stop crying some days. She would put her arm around me and tell me it was all going to be okay.

I can show my love towards my children more freely, now I have escaped my Dominator. I shout less at my children now, because I am less stressed. We have so much more fun, and we laugh so much more than we did before. I do silly things with them now, and am not so serious about everything. We can be noisy when we wake up in the morning, and I don't have to keep telling them shush. We have music on loud, and dance. We chill out together on the sofa, and watch a film. We would never dream of doing that when I was with my abuser.

Most of all, I actually do love them more than I ever did. This makes me feel quite guilty, but, looking back, it was difficult to love them when I had to survive day-by-day with him, and was worrying about what he might say or do. Now, it is just us, we are happy. It is hard work being a single mum, but life is just easy compared to life with My Dominator! I will never be free of him, because of the links with the children, but thanks to the Freedom Programme I can see through all his tactics and this makes me feel liberated.

The Freedom Programme

Doing the sessions on the Effects on the Children really scared me. I saw my future and the futures of my children if I stayed with him. I looked around the room, and listened to the experiences of other women whose children were older, and all the issues the children had. I knew I had made the right decision to leave him now, whilst the children were young. I read, somewhere, that children who witness domestic violence are experiencing child abuse. In the end, I left my abuser for the sake of the children. It took me several months of being free to realise that, actually, it was for the sake of me, too.

It took me a long time to have the courage to leave my abuser, but, after 18 months of freedom, I am so happy and feel so free. Most importantly, my children are going to grow up to be confident, independent and loving individuals with a strong, independent role model of a mother...

Sunflower

…It took Pat Craven's wonderful **Freedom Programme** and book **'Living with the Dominator'** to make me realise that, although I had not been physically abused by my husbands and partners, I *had never been free of my father*.

I had been psychologically, emotionally and verbally assaulted by all the men I had relationships with. I also found out that the men who told me I was too fat, thin, stupid, thick, ugly, sexless, who lied to me, who had affairs, with one husband having a child with his secretary, were just 'versions of my father'.

He had been in my psyche, and fertile in my choice of partners, for all my life.

Since the Freedom Programme, I now know '*I really didn't know*' how to live my life differently. I was completely unaware that I only married, or had relationships with, my father. Now, with this new education and awareness, I have a future where I can choose to have healthy and happy relationships, filled with honesty, integrity and love…

Starflower

… I have woken today feeling really guilty, as I must confess that when I was in the midst of the abusive relationship, suffering multiple verbal onslaughts a day, I would regularly walk away, in relief, if he turned on the children instead of me. I am not proud of what I did, but, at the time, it was just a relief not to be in the firing line myself. If I stepped in to defend them, he turned on me instead, so, sometimes, when feeling weak, I simply walked away. One incident, just before I left, is etched onto my brain. For some reason, he kicked off at Daughter 1 who was in the kitchen on the laptop. He was cooking, and being absorbed in what she was doing, she had probably not answered a question quickly enough. So he clouted her round the head from behind with a pack of frozen Yorkshire puddings. The poor kid did not see it coming, and, to my shame, I walked out of the room.

Living in that intensely charged, mentally and emotionally abusive, environment with physical outbursts, made me very anxious and short-tempered. It isn't, really, until now that I have some space, that I have realised just how insanely fractious and angry I had become, and how abnormal the living situation was. I, occasionally, had temper "melt downs" where I screamed at the children so loudly I made my throat sore and went puce.

These episodes scared me as they were not "me", and I was ashamed that I reacted so irrationally and totally inappropriately to a misdemeanour.

He has now been gone three whole months, and my mood is much more even, I can stay calm for much longer and discuss or argue more reasonably with the children. Previously I would take things out on them. I would turn and snap at them for trivial things. I was so wound up, all the time, through walking on eggshells that it took very little to make me react. In the same way, the children, too, living on eggshells, had very short fuses, and the change from calm to fury, with no warning or gradual build up, was like a switch being flicked.

With hindsight, I can liken the way we were living as being like four caged tigers, all on permanent high alert, ready to defend ourselves at the slightest provocation.

Since his departure, I can honestly say life has improved dramatically. I can parent in my own way, without him contradicting decisions. We have all had to make adjustments. New boundaries have, obviously, been pushed and tested, and, in some cases, moved to accommodate the new circumstances. Thankfully, harmony has mostly been restored! The permanent anxiety and nausea I felt in my stomach has melted away, and my health has begun to improve, so I can only suppose that the same holds true for the children.

The arguments the children have with me have declined, both in number and intensity, from several a day to, possibly, one a week, or fortnight. The children are still bickering and flaring up at each other, but not at their former intensity, volume, or for the same duration. The children no longer have to ask if their dad will be coming home at night, and then behave according to my response. So they are noisier round the house, singing and dancing, playing music and laughing. They are also saying, "thank you" spontaneously more regularly, and are telling me they love me.

The next milestone will be to see when they ask to have friends round to stay. I have suggested they have a couple of mates over, but, as yet, they have not taken up the offer. Maybe they are viewing home as a sanctuary now he has gone, alternatively it could, simply, be that, as yet, they are ashamed of it, because it has so much half-done DIY there is not one completed room!...

My reply to Starflower

Dearest Starflower

Never forget that you have saved them by getting rid of him. You did it when you could and, if you could have done it sooner, you would have done.

Apple Blossom

… Culturally, a bad man is better than no man. However, I did not give in to cultural and societal demands! My children will learn though my experiences.

"Rich gifts wax poor when givers prove unkind."

I know I can succeed in my life now. I have found two new social work positions, and I love being a working, emancipated mother again. Instead of self-medicating, I now live a healthy, contented and happy life. I have a future.

Life is looking good again, and I have to thank you, Pat, for your support. It gave me hope and maintained my integrity, despite all the madness (at times I could not sleep, and was going through a form of visual psychosis).

Simply, Thanks to the Freedom Programme…

Rose

….How the Freedom Programme has changed my life.

I first read 'Living with the Dominator' when a support worker for my son gave it to me. Although I was no longer living with my husband, he was still very much in my life, and still governing my every move. Although I was no longer physically living with him, I was still emotionally attached, and he was exploiting this at every opportunity he could.

I read the book in one evening, and the impression it left on me was colossal. I could not put the book down! I kept reading it over and over again, scrutinising every sentence, separating every word. My whole life was unravelling in front of me on, each page of the book.

For as long as I could remember, I made countless excuses for this man. I had several professionals work with me, dear family members appeal to me, and friends plead with me. The justification I used to others and, of course, to myself was that it did not matter, because he loved me. Yet, when I read this book, I saw, for the very first time, that he did not, indeed, love me, but was controlling me!!

That was the beginning for me. I was slowly able to grasp the concept that our marriage was not based on love, but based on control. I made small steps, I emotionally disentangled myself from him and, inwardly, I began to become free and, at last, find peace.

Not long after, I went on a Freedom Programme. Being able to share intimate moments of pain with others who I could relate to was, to me, liberating. Making connections with others, and reviewing his tactics, gave me the courage and determination to stay free from him. I could now see him exactly as he was, a Dominator. I was then able to become physically free from him, putting into place the measures needed.

Now, my life is a very different life. I have learnt the true meaning of love, and began to love myself. Slow small steps at first, like taking hot warm bubble baths, reading books, having pj days. Doing everything I could never do when I was with him. I had counselling, and built up my self-esteem. I kept reading as much as I could, and constantly referred back to the Freedom Book when I had low moments. I had fun and new relationships, using the Freedom Book to look for warning signs of potential Dominators.

The biggest change was the quality of life my children were, now, able to have. Empower the mother and you empower the children. I was able to play, educate and discipline my children. I could do none of these things when the Dominator was in our lives. I was able to use the work in the book to show the children how a healthy adult behaves.

This book, this programme, has changed my life and my five children's lives. I will never, ever be able to repay Pat for what she has done.

I just wanted to share something lovely that happen this morning. I was feeling a little sorry for myself, and slightly manic after a week of attending countless mental health appointments for my oldest son, when I drove past a face I remembered.

I stopped the car, and it was the very lady who first gave me the 'Living with the Dominator' book. She was my son's support worker. How wonderful it was to tell her how this book, which led me to the programme, had changed my life! She also loves the book. My perspective for the day very quickly changed when

I remembered how different my life was, when I first knew her.
I love life now, thanks to the Freedom Programme!

"OUR LIVES ARE SO MUCH BETTER NOW MUMMY"...

Appendix

Murdered children

I have years of experience in dealing with violent and abusive men.
I have learned that they always plan to use violence and that it is never
spontaneous. They can decide to murder days, months or years before
they actually do it. They kill children to punish their mother for ending
the relationship. Sometimes, this is obvious to courts and reports.
On other occasions, it is only obvious to Freedom Programme people.

Telegraph – 13 December 2011

Murdered family in Leeds had been stabbed, say police

A mother and her two young sons found dead at their house in Leeds
had been stabbed, police said today.

Clair Smith, 36, and her sons Ben, nine, and Aaron, one, are thought to
have been attacked by the boys' father Richard Smith, 37, who died of
smoke inhalation after killing them.

Mr Smith, the coach of a junior football team, is believed to have killed
his wife and two young children before setting their bodies on fire and
committing suicide.

The four bodies were found in an upstairs bedroom of the family home
in Sheridan Way, Pudsey, near Leeds, on Sunday after concerned
relatives raised the alarm.

Independent - 12 December 2011

A father who killed his two children by cutting their throats while they lay in bed, as an act of revenge against his estranged wife, was told yesterday that he would serve a minimum of 30 years in prison.

Jean Say, 62, a retired concierge, originally from Ivory Coast, was facing eviction as a result of bitter separation from his wife, Antoinette, and killed the couple's children while they were on a weekend visit to his London flat.

After Say killed daughter Regina, eight, and son Rolls, 10, he rang his wife to say: "I have killed your children. Come and get the bodies."

Daily Mail - 25 May 2012

Bodies of woman and three young children found in burning home early Tuesday morning

Body of man found 75 miles away in red SUV

Police believe victims were killed before house was set alight

A mother and her three young children were found dead in a burned house, and the children's father was later found dead in a car 75 miles away in what police believe to be a murder-suicide.

Police said the bodies of the woman and children were discovered early Tuesday in a Salem, Oregon home, while the father was found dead in a hotel parking lot about 75 miles away in Cottage Grove.

The victims weren't immediately identified, though police said that they died. The woman and children were discovered early Tuesday when

95

Salem fire fighters responded to a house fire located in the 2800 block of Fisher Road Northeast.

'As fire fighters were attending to the fire in the residence, they located the three young children and the woman and removed them from the house,' said Lieutenant Dave Okada, a spokesman for the Salem Police Department.

'Evidence located at the scene indicated that the victims died as a result of homicidal violence and fire fighters requested the Salem Police Department respond.'

A neighbour reported awaking about 5:30 a.m. to the fire.

Dan Grove told the Salem Statesman Journal that he 'saw dark, black smoke pouring out of the house. I heard people screaming and yelling. It was for real.'

About five hours later, the father was found dead in a vehicle about 75 miles south of Salem, in Cottage Grove.

Mail Online - Saturday Jul 14 2012

Report by Kevin Toolis

Gunned down: Maisie Copland was shot by her father

Father kills his four children. Dad executes four-year-old girl. The headlines scream off the page and a shiver of apprehension runs through every mother's mind.

In the latest family annihilation, just after Christmas, 56-year-old Andrew Copland waited at his Hampshire home for his former partner

Julie Harrison to drop off their four-year-old daughter Maisie for an access visit to open her Christmas presents.

In our divorce-ridden society there was nothing unusual about this awkward Christmas ritual, as estranged parents nationwide share what's left of their children's belief in Santa Claus. But once Julie and Maisie were in his house, Copland pulled a gun and shot them both before turning the weapon on himself.

How could a father kill his child? It is a crime that defies our comprehension. Your own flesh and blood? There is a word - filicide - for this act of homicide. But we rarely use it, perhaps because we find such acts too horrible to name.

Andrew Copland had a history of violence against his partners. He was a jealous man with few friends, and his relationship with Julie had been troubled. But, tragically, his crime was not unique.

About 10 per cent of all the homicides in Britain each year are child killings. In an average year, 75 children will be murdered, the vast majority by their own parents or step-parents. Despite our fears of 'stranger danger', only a handful of children are actually abducted and murdered by people unknown to them.

Independent - Monday 14 February 2011

Mother and two children found dead after father kills himself

A man is believed to have murdered his family before killing himself, after four bodies were discovered in Leicester over the weekend.

Aram Abdul Razaq Aziz was found dead at Watermead Country Park on Friday evening, before the bodies of his former partner and their two small children were uncovered on Saturday morning.

Joy Small, 24, was found together with their three-year-old son Aubarr Aziz and two-year-old daughter Chanarra in their flat on Jersey Road, around two miles from the park.

The causes of their deaths have not yet been ascertained, and Leicestershire Police were keen to underline that their enquiries are still at an early stage. But with neighbours speaking of Mr Aziz having a tempestuous and sometimes violent relationship with Ms Small, in which the police had previously been involved, a spokesman for the constabulary said they were not looking for anyone else in connection with the deaths.

A spokesman for Leicestershire Police said: "Officers are investigating the circumstances that led to the deaths of all four. No causes of death have been established at present. Post mortem examinations are due to be held [today]. The deaths of the woman and children are being treated as suspicious."

While local residents spoke of their shock at what had happened, Jennie Bland, a 27-year-old neighbour and friend of Ms Small's, described Mr Aziz as an "abusive monster".

Miss Bland said that Ms Small had got a panic button installed after breaking up with Mr Aziz, and that the young mother had kept the fact they later got back together a secret, as she feared her children might be taken away for their safety.

"I knew what he was like," she said. "I met him a few times, he didn't like me because Joy could be herself when she was around me. She got back with him after being so strong after he poured petrol on her and tried to set her alight. He beat her all the time, the time he poured petrol on her he threw a mirror at her son. He tried to stop her seeing her friends, that's why he didn't like me.

Miss Bland added: "We fell out because she got back with him. I couldn't just sit back and let it happen, I should have just gone on my instincts and told the police and social services." She paid tribute to her friend as "a fantastic mum".

Other neighbours left flowers and cuddly toys outside the flat.

Mirror - 9 December 2011

Ex-policeman kills wife and child before committing suicide

Two teenagers were being treated for serious injuries today after their former police officer father killed their mother and sister before killing himself.

Neighbours said Tobias Day had recently lost his police job.

He killed his wife Samantha and his seven-year-old daughter Genevieve, and attacked his two other children Kimberly and Adam before taking his own life yesterday.

The incident, in a quiet residential street in Melton Mowbray in Leicestershire, left neighbours horrified.

Police officers were seen going in and out of the Days' house on Robin Crescent this morning.

Leicestershire Police refused to comment on suggestions that Day had recently lost his job as an inspector.

Police said they received a report at around 4.23pm yesterday that a 15-year-old girl, believed to be Kimberly, had been injured in Melton Mowbray.

She was taken to hospital and during the investigation officers forced their way into the family's house, where they discovered two children and two adults with injuries.

The force later confirmed that a man, a woman and a child had died, and two other children were being treated at the Queen's Medical Centre in Nottingham with serious injuries.

Officers were seen this morning entering nearby Swallowdale Primary School, where Mrs Day worked as a teacher.

Neighbour Samantha Whitfield, who has lived on Robin Crescent with her husband for around 15 years, said she was shocked over the attack.

"Its usually a quiet street," she said. "I've never seen anything like this.

"When we saw all the police and ambulances yesterday, we knew something had happened."

"I think she worked at the nursery as a teacher.

"They were a normal family from what I saw. I didn't see him too much."

She said her two children had been scared by the events.

BBC News - 30 March 2010

A father who made a farewell video of his two children before strangling them has been jailed for life after being convicted of their murders.

Petros Williams killed Yolanda Molemohi, four, and two-year-old Theo Molemohi at his flat in Whalley Range, Manchester, last October.

In the video, shown to Manchester Crown Crown, Williams, 37, urged the children to say goodbye to their mother.

He has been told he will serve a minimum of 28 years in prison.

Mr Justice Parker, sentencing, said it was hard to conceive any more shocking crime.

The court was told that Zimbabwe-born Williams deliberately chose internet connection cords to choke the children to punish his wife for using dating websites after the breakdown of their marriage.

'Terrifying moments'

His wife, Morongoe Molemohi, 30, had started using the websites to see other men, the jury was told.

Andrew Thomas QC, prosecuting, said he killed the children as a symbolic act of punishment to his wife.

Ms Molehomi discovered the bodies of her children in Williams' one-bedroom flat.

Her estranged husband was lying beside them dazed, but uninjured, next to a noose.

Ms Molehomi said in a statement after the hearing: "I will never be able to wipe the image from my mind, nor forget the terrifying desperate moments when I scrambled to help them, to call for help from others and to do what I could for them while I waited for the emergency services to arrive.

"Try to imagine the panic, the isolation and the sense of uselessness in those moments, as I realised that my most precious children needed me the most and I was unable to save them."

'Bye Mummy'

The video tape found in the flat shows the children sitting in the living room with Williams initially behind the camera before he joined them on the sofa and told them: "Say, 'bye Mummy'."

The tape was labelled, "Daddy, Yolly, Theo. Byee The End".

There was a note attached which said, "Play the video, made for your memories, thank you, Petros".

Williams, who had denied two counts of murder, was found guilty by the jury after 90 minutes of deliberation.

He had tried to blame his wife for the killings, but the judge said there was "no doubt" he had intended to kill them.

"It is hard to conceive any more shocking crime than a parent deliberately taking the life of his or her child," said Mr Justice Parker.

"We saw from the video that Yolanda and Theo were happy children, full of love and laughter, with a whole lifetime ahead of them and, above all, absolute trust in their father who, for entirely selfish purposes, would end their brief lives."

London Evening Standard – 20 January 2012

Met detectives could face disciplinary action for failing to investigate a rape allegation that may have jailed a father before he murdered his two children.

Retired security guard Jean Say was jailed for life last month after he admitted stabbing to death daughter Regina, eight, and 10-year-old son Rolls with a carving knife during an access visit to his flat in Southwark.

The Old Bailey heard that he was a "jealous, controlling bully" who had previously threatened to do something the whole world would talk about, and that he carried out the killing to spite his estranged wife, Adjoua.

He had continued to visit his children despite a history of domestic violence and an alleged assault on his wife which had led to a non-molestation order.

Maxinews.co.uk – 25 April 2011

The French police have sought the help of policemen around the world to help them arrest a 50-year-old father who reportedly killed his own wife and three children in the northern city of Nantes in France.

The French police has issued an international search alert for murder suspect Xavier Dupont de Ligonnes amid evidence that he carefully planned the killing of his wife and four children.

It can be recalled that the bodies of the victims who bore gun shot wounds were recovered at a grave beneath their house in the said area.

Nantes public prosecutor Xavier Ronsin said initial police investigation tagged Xavier Dupont, the father as the most likely culprit in the killing and also may be involved in last week's disappearance of a woman in the southeastern Var region.

According to reports, Dupont was last spotted on April 15 in the region, hundreds of miles (kilometers) from the family home where the bodies of his four children, aged 13-21, and 49-year-old wife were found.

Autopsies done on the bodies showed the victims had been "methodically" shot with a .22 calibre firearm, similar to one that Dupont de Ligonnes had used in shooting practice at a Nantes rifle club.

Wife Agnes, 49, daughter Anne, 16, and three sons were apparently shot several times in the head while asleep, around April 3 or 4, and tests are under way to see if they were drugged first.

Ronsin revealed the mother and the children had been shot in the head, possibly with a rifle belonging to Dupont.

He said the family went missing in early April.

London Evening Standard - 9 March 2007

Perry Samuel suffocated his two children as revenge on their mother who he feared was cheating on him, a court heard today.

Perry Samuel, 35, held his hands over the mouths and noses of his five-year-old daughter, Caitlin, and her brother, Aiden, three, until they lost consciousness and died.

In a vain bid to make their murders look like an accident, Samuel then dumped their naked bodies in the bath and rang 999, telling police: 'There's a problem with the children.'

Officers arrested Samuel at the terrace home he shared with the children's mother, 23-year-old Sarah Graham, who was away at a pop concert at the time, shortly afterwards.

He was questioned for three days but repeatedly refused to explain why he had murdered the children.

Daily Mail – 21 February 2009

Man who killed himself and his two children left 'Bitch' note rigged up to homemade bomb for his wife

A father killed his two young children and then committed suicide after a bitter marriage breakdown, an inquest heard yesterday.

Brian Philcox, 53, even left a boobytrap bomb in his home, designed to explode as his wife opened a note he had left, addressed to the 'Bitch'. But it failed to detonate.

The horror happened on Father's Day weekend in June last year.

Philcox's children Amy, seven and Owen, three, had been spending a day with him as one of their regular contact visits.

They were excitedly clutching home-made Father's Day cards as he picked them up from the home of his estranged wife Lyn McAuliffe on Friday.

Security guard Philcox, from Runcorn, Cheshire, had been supposed to return them on Saturday evening.

Instead, he drove his Land Rover to a remote beauty spot in the heart of Snowdonia in North Wales.

Philcox had sedated the children with drugs and makeshift chloroform masks.

He climbed into the back seat with them as exhaust fumes filled the car, killing all three. Police found their bodies the following day.

The Llandudno inquest heard that Philcox, a karate expert, had married Miss McAuliffe in 2000. But they split over his violent and controlling personality and were involved in an acrimonious divorce.

Amy Philcox, seven, and her three-year-old brother Owen were found dead in a Land Rover on Father's Day last year. Their father had poisoned them with carbon monoxide fumes

Miss McAuliffe was claiming possession of the family home, but Philcox had told a friend: 'That woman wants everything - my house and my money and my kids.

'She's trying to take me to the cleaners and leave me with nothing - well I'm not going to let her.'

Miss McAuliffe told the inquest that Philcox had sent a text message on the evening he was supposed to return the children, saying he was having trouble with the car.

He later phoned and repeatedly apologised to her.

She said: ' He kept saying: "There's nothing I can do, it is out of my control, I am sorry".

'He threw me because I didn't know then what he was talking about. I thought he was talking about the car.'

At 10.45pm he sent another text telling her to get his spare key and enter his house.

Miss McAuliffe called police and her sister Geraldine Craven went round to the property. Inside, she found an envelope with the word 'Bitch' written on it. It had been glued to a kitchen work top.

Police later realised that the act of ripping it off was supposed to spark an explosion from elaborate devices Philcox had hidden in his walls, skirting boards and under the kitchen table. But they failed to go off.

Police launched a major hunt for Philcox and the children. They were finally found dead on the afternoon of Father's Day.

Home Office pathologist Brian Rodgers told the inquest the children's bodies showed no signs of injury or struggle. They would have been deeply asleep before the carbon monoxide fumes killed them.

Miss McAuliffe, of Runcorn, sat in tears through the hearing.

Afterwards, in a statement read out by her sister, Miss McAuliffe said: 'Since Amy and Owen died, my life has been a constant nightmare. I don't feel as if I have been coping - just existing. No day is easy without them.

'Some people have mentioned that maybe someday, I or we as a family, will forgive Brian. I will never forgive him for taking our beautiful Amy and Owen.

'He had no right to take their lives. He was an evil man whose attempts to use homemade bombs clearly show that all his acts were that of a cold-blooded, premeditated killer.'

Philcox had contacted the pressure group Fathers 4 Justice to tell them of his desperation over the divorce. After the tragedy, the group was disbanded by founder Matt O'Connor, who said: 'People intimated we were somehow responsible for his actions.

'I had a two-minute conversation with him, I had no idea that was what he was going to do. I felt I had become responsible for the behaviour of every father.'

The Guardian - Tuesday 23 September 2008

A man who is believed to have smothered his two young daughters while they were on a weekend custody visit telephoned their mother to say "the children have gone to sleep forever" before killing himself, it emerged last night.

The man, named locally as David Cass, 32, was found dead on Sunday evening with his two children, Ellie aged three, and Isobel, one, in a caravan parked at the Southampton garage where he worked. Cass separated from the children's mother, Kerry Hughes, four months ago and since then had intermittently slept in the caravan, parked at Paynes Road Car Sales.

At the weekend, he was caring for the youngsters for the first time after an acrimonious split with Hughes. He picked the children up on Saturday morning and was due to return them to their mother when he called her at around 6.45pm.

A family friend, Val Frasier, said last night: "He apparently said to her, 'The children have gone to sleep forever and I'm going to hang myself'."

Hughes called Hampshire police immediately after receiving the call, but when officers forced open the gates of the garage the three were already dead. A police spokesman said they were not looking for anyone else in connection with the deaths.

Earlier in the week, Cass is thought to have been confident of winning custody of his daughters. The garage's manager, John Martin, described how Cass's mood had changed after his hopes about custody arrangements for the children were dashed.

"On Friday morning he was ecstatic with it all - he said it all looked good and he thought he could get back into the house and have custody of the kids. But that obviously went pear-shaped somewhere," he added.

By Friday afternoon, Martin said, Cass was "depressed and angry" and handed his notice in to the garage, claiming he had a plan. Martin said he urged him "not to do anything stupid".

"I thought he would go back and cause havoc round the house and get himself arrested. I didn't realise he was going to be that desperate," he said.

The garage's owner, John Mayhew, said he saw Cass on Saturday and described him as "very, very low". "He worked on Saturday until 1pm. He was depressed. He said it was something to do with the custody of his children. He was a nice lad. He was a very good worker. He kept himself to himself, he was mellow. He was a doting father -it sounds ridiculous, but he was a doting father."

Hughes was too distraught to talk, but a friend, Emma Timberlake, paid tribute to the young girls: "Ellie's laugh made everyone smile because it was so cute. I was on the phone to Kerry on Friday and I could hear Izzy and Ellie laughing and having a play fight. And then Ellie started tickling her mother and I was thinking how cute that was.

"Ellie was a gorgeous little girl, and Kerry used to call her the ginger ninja. Izzy was so beautiful when she was born and she had just started to become the gorgeous little girl that Ellie was."

The incident has led to renewed calls for a Samaritans-style helpline for fathers locked in custody battles. Members of the now disbanded campaign group Fathers 4 Justice said the number of contacts from desperate parents pleading for advice had surged.

The case is the latest in a number of incidents this year in which fathers have killed their children. Last month, failed businessman Christopher Foster is believed to have shot his teenage daughter and his wife before setting fire to the family's home in Shropshire and killing himself.
In June, Brian Philox gassed himself and his two young children while on a Father's Day outing to Snowdonia.

Mail Online – 3 April 2009

Millionaire Christopher Foster murdered his wife Jill and daughter Kirstie, 15, before committing suicide, a coroner ruled yesterday.

Mr Foster shot his family and their pet dogs and horses before setting his £1.2million mansion ablaze in August last year. Earlier, the court had been shown the last actions of Mr Foster, caught on CCTV security cameras on the night of the blaze, as he walked around the grounds of his home in Oswestry, Shropshire, carrying what is thought to be a bucket, a rifle and a battery pack in preparation for setting the fire.

It also heard how Kirstie had spent the final moments before her death texting a friend, with no indication of the horror that lay ahead.

'Foster kept guns all over the house. And his targets included Jill's doves when they got into the garage and left droppings on his cars. He also shot Kirstie's pet Labrador when it worried sheep and the angry farmer threatened to shoot it himself.

Kirstie was very upset, and his friends were shocked he hadn't given it away or let a vet put it down. But they describe him as 'like Jekyll and Hyde' - very charming and attractive, but also headstrong, and impulsive. When in 'one of his moods', Jill would steer clear of him.'

The Guardian – 22 November 2008

'Along with the mansion and the cars, there were the affairs. Foster had at least eight mistresses, according to Jill's sister, Anne Giddings. "He had a big thing about blondes," Giddings later told the Sunday People. "Jill knew all about his affairs. There were lots of women on the scene. But she played the dutiful wife and kept quiet. He wasn't a good-looking guy, but money did the talking. He was always flashing the cash - it seemed to give him confidence."

The Guardian - Thursday 24 January 2008

Cleared of murder: father who leapt off balcony with children

Natasha Hogan needed 10 minutes to compose herself properly after the verdict was read out. Even then, she couldn't read the statement she had written, though her words left nobody in any doubt about her feelings towards her ex-husband, and their six-year-old son, whom he had killed.

"It has left me feeling that Liam lost his young life for nothing," she said. "I accept that an act in a moment of complete madness was uncharacteristic of John, but to have done this to our children is unforgivable. I know that we all miss Liam but it is [my daughter] Mia and I that are left to rebuild our lives without a loving, caring son and brother."

That moment of complete madness came on August 15 2006, when John Hogan jumped 50 feet from a four-storey hotel balcony holding his son and two-year-old daughter.

The rebuilding of Mrs Hogan's life will continue in the UK, while Hogan, cleared of murder, was ordered into specialist treatment in Greece, though his doctor thought this may not take long.

Last night his psychiatrist, Professor Ioannes Nestoros, said: "If he goes to a good hospital and has good psychotherapy maybe he could leave in about a year's time as an outpatient."

The order to send Hogan into hospital care came at the end of an emotional two-day trial in which he had claimed to have no recollection of jumping from the balcony shortly after his wife had told him she wanted a divorce.

As the verdict was returned at the criminal court in Chania yesterday, Hogan, 33, gasped "I'm innocent" and burst into tears.

Across the courtroom, Mrs Hogan slumped and held her head in her hands.

As he was led from court in handcuffs, he was asked if he was pleased with the verdict. "How can I be pleased when my son is dead?" he replied.

A jury of three judges and four lay people ruled that Hogan should be hospitalised indefinitely until doctors conclude he is no longer a danger to himself or his family. Speaking in a slurred voice caused by his dosage of anti-depressants, he had insisted that one day "I will be a father to my daughter again". He told the judges and jurors on the bench: "I feel no guilt because I did not do it.

"This person you see before you is not the person who jumped from the fourth floor. I already have my son's forgiveness and God's forgiveness."

Paraskevi Kiraleou, the presiding judge, said after a deliberation that lasted 40 minutes: "His responsibility was diminished. He was incapable of murdering his son and he needs to be in a psychiatric unit for therapy."

Hogan's defence lawyer, Dimitris Xyritakis, said last night: "He is not guilty but they think that he must be kept for a short period in a hospital, because they think he is a danger to himself and others. He is very happy. All his members of the family are with him. This is the right verdict. He is now a prisoner of doctors not of police and judges."

The court's decision turned on whether the judges believed Hogan was psychotic at the time of the incident.

Yesterday he set out to persuade the jury that he was a loving father who had been driven mad by his wife's decision to leave him.

Breaking down in tears in front of the judge, he said: "I have never loved three people more than my ex-wife and my two children. They were the world to me ... I was the best dad those children could have. Every time I was with them we did something special, take them to a park, take them swimming, take them to a farm."

The incident, the court heard, happened during a "make-or-break" holiday for Hogan and his wife. They had flown with their children to the beachside Petra Mare hotel in Ierpetra, on Crete's south coast.

Their marriage was on the brink of collapse and Mrs Hogan was already investigating divorce procedures. Their relationship was closer to that of brother and sister than husband and wife, Hogan said.

Their sex life lacked emotional intimacy, he complained.
The marriage had been in trouble for several years.

Hogan had once threatened to burn down the family home in Bradley Stoke, Gloucestershire, if they ever split up and the couple went on a similar holiday to Prague to try to save the marriage in 2003.

During the trial Mrs Hogan was questioned about "flirty" emails which Hogan had discovered in 2005 and she said they had talked about divorce, but he had not been able to accept the prospect.

Four days into the holiday, Mrs Hogan told her husband she planned to divorce him when they returned home. Hogan insisted they should leave immediately and made arrangements for flights home through the travel agent First Choice. But he could only arrange for three tickets. That triggered a furious row in the hotel room over who should accompany the children. Each insisted it should be them.

"I was in a panic, in a state of distress," said Hogan. "I thought that I was going to lose everything ... What I was trying to do [over] those four days was make somebody love me that didn't love me."

He said his final memories before plunging from the hotel balcony were sitting with Liam sleeping in one arm and Mia on his other arm.

Again and again Judge Kiraleou and prosecutor Helena Papanikolopoulou pressed him to recall his jump and every time he replied: "I can't remember."

He said: "I jumped over a wall, I had my children in my arms. I don't remember. A sane John Hogan would not have done what he did that night so please don't judge me for that one incident and if there is any way I could bring my son back I would."

Mrs Hogan's version was different. She said she made a disparaging remark about how he was packing his case and Mr Hogan reacted angrily and had "a crazed look in his eye". Moments later, he jumped.

"The next thing I saw was Liam, just lying there in a heap," she said. "I just went into nurse mode. I couldn't see his injuries. I was looking at his face thinking 'ABC. I want you to live. ABC - airways, breathing, circulation. Let's concentrate on this.' I knew he was dying. I glanced at John. He was over to the right and I thought he was dead. I thought, 'Good. Fine. Just leave him alone and concentrate on my son.' "

Hogan said he was hallucinating in the ambulance immediately after the incident. In interviews with his psychiatrist he also said he believed he was on the ground floor at the hotel and could simply walk out with his children and that he was taking them "to paradise".

The Hogan family has a history of tragedy and severe mental health problems. Hogan was prescribed medication and psychotherapy to treat panic attacks prior to the incident.

Two of his brothers, Stephen and Paul, killed themselves. When he was 17, Stephen killed himself shortly after the death of his father from multiple sclerosis. Paul, who suffered from manic depression, leapt from a bridge in Bristol in 2004.

Hogan's elder sister, Gabrielle, said John was the man everyone came to rely on in her family after the death of their father.

Hogan had tried to kill himself at least four times since his arrest.

"My son was in paradise in heaven," Hogan said in court explaining his suicide attempts. "I wanted to be there, cuddle him, put an arm round him and tell him how sorry I am."

He will continue his treatment in a hospital in Athens and was due to take a ferry to the mainland today.

Mrs Hogan, an accident and emergency nurse, has married Richard Visser, 41, a former colleague. She said yesterday that she was planning to rebuild her family's life away from the media spotlight. There were reports she may start a new life in Australia.

Mail Online – 17 December 2007

My husband murdered our children

Fourteen years after her vengeful husband strangled their two young children to 'punish' her for their broken marriage, Sarah Heatley is still living with the grief of an unimaginable act of cruelty – and campaigning for changes to a legal system that failed to put the safety of her children before their father's rights of access.

Sarah Heatley is perched on a stool in the kitchen of her Worcestershire home, sipping coffee. The dog is at her feet and Sarah's 12-year-old son George is playing outside. The scene is one of domestic ordinariness, but it is also an illusion.

"I may look normal," Sarah says. "But I don't feel normal, and I don't suppose I ever will."

It is nearly 14 years since Sarah's life was irrevocably changed by the deaths of her first two children, Nina, four, and Jack, three.

They were killed in the most abhorrent way imaginable at the hands of their father, who strangled them with their pyjama cords.

Sarah Heatley now campaigns for changes to the legal system to prioritise childrens' safety

"It was a Sunday morning. They would have been awake, and he put their pyjama jackets over their faces, so I guess he couldn't bear to see them die. I know that he couldn't have killed both of them at the same time, so one child knew what was coming. And that makes me feel really ill," she says, her grip tightening on her coffee mug.

To the outside world, Sarah's husband Dave, a GP, was an upstanding member of the community. To Sarah, however, he had become a violent, vengeful husband. She had left him six months earlier after enduring mental and physical abuse and, as he became increasingly unstable, she had argued vehemently against him being allowed unsupervised access to their children.

Instead of being heard, she was painted as an over-reactive mother. A court welfare officer described her as 'intransigent'; her barrister told her that if she objected, the court would allow him to spend time alone with the children anyway.

On three occasions, Dave had access visits with Nina and Jack. "And I was afraid every time," Sarah recalls. "He had started to do things deliberately to provoke me, such as not strapping them in the car. Nina would say: 'We don't wear seat belts with Daddy because you don't like that.' It had got to the point where his hatred towards me was greater than his love for our children. I knew deep down they were in grave danger."

One of her fears was that he would abduct them. "He used to say, 'You'll never keep them from me. I will take them somewhere where you will never see them again.' I misinterpreted that. I now realise that he had it in his mind to kill them all along. It was his trump card."

Of all crimes, those in which a parent takes the lives of their own trusting children are surely the most heinous. The deaths of Nina and Jack caused shockwaves, as did the death of their father, whose body was found hours later at the bottom of a block of flats.

And Sarah's is not a unique tragedy. Every year, stories emerge of fathers who commit similarly devastating killings. We comb the details for evidence that will enable us to detach them from our own reality ? a mental illness, perhaps, or some other underlying reason.
And then we move on.

It says much, therefore, for Sarah's tenacity and determination that she refuses to let her story be forgotten. In the years since her children's murder, she has been relentless in her efforts to secure a radical shift of thinking within our legal system. She has taken part in television documentaries, met with the Lord Chancellor's office, and worked with the NSPCC and Women's Aid, the national charity specialising in domestic violence.

Three years ago, she contributed to a Women's Aid report, entitled Twenty-Nine Child Homicides: Lessons Still to be Learnt on Domestic Violence and Child Protection. It calls for the safety of children to be paramount and for court professionals to be held accountable, so that those who make decisions which put children in danger can be overruled or struck off.

On one wall of Sarah's kitchen, shelves display photographs of Nina and Jack, frozen in time, and pictures of George, her now-only child from a long-dissolved relationship. There are pictures, too, of Sarah, taking part in various marathons. Slight and sinewy, physically; mentally she displays remarkable endurance.

Now 43, Sarah grew up in the Midlands, one of four daughters from a close family. Her innate compassion and capacity for hard work made her ideal for her chosen career of nursing. In 1987 she met her future husband while working at Queen Mary's Hospital in Roehampton, West London. She was 23 and a staff nurse; he was 28 and a junior doctor on her ward.

"He was clever, a high achiever, impossible to dislike," she remembers. They fell for each other instantly and within 12 months Sarah became pregnant with Nina. They married and Jack followed shortly afterwards. Her family were quick to embrace Dave.

"He was bright, funny, special and our kids were special too ? not too good, not too naughty, but balanced and spot on."

By 1992, Dave was a GP in Derbyshire, Sarah was a nursing sister in a research unit, and home was a four-bedroomed house set in an acre of garden. But just as they appeared to have achieved the middle-class dream, cracks emerged.

Stressed by work and financial burdens, Dave became possessive and controlling. He gave Sarah a cheque book, but no bank cards, and just enough cash to get her to work and back. She became adept at peace-keeping.

"If he said, 'I want a cup of tea,' he got a cup of tea. He would tell me, 'Don't go near the children.' And I would stand back. He was showing behaviour I had never seen, but I made allowances because I didn't want our children to be brought up in a broken marriage."

Sarah's feisty demeanour betrays none of the subservience you would expect to find in a victim of domestic violence. "I was one of those who used to say: 'Nobody will hit me more than once.' And I'll tell you, it comes as a hell of a shock when it does happen. But by then, I was trapped. That is how these men do it. They control you financially and emotionally before they come in with the thumps."

Dave was more than 6ft tall and 15 stone. Sarah weighed less than half that. One night, in May 1993, he came home, sat on her chest, and pounded her repeatedly about the head with his fists until her nose bled and her eyes were black.

He had been drinking, but was not drunk and, unlike some abusers, showed no remorse afterwards. Three months later, when he threatened to beat her up again, and this time kill her, Sarah left, aided by her parents and a police escort. Dave's mental state rapidly deteriorated.

He was signed off work and referred to a psychiatrist. He stalked Sarah relentlessly; she took out injunctions. "My plan wasn't to keep him away from the children indefinitely, but to keep him away until he calmed down."

A court welfare officer was given ten weeks to assess their case. Sarah, it was suggested, as "making her husband's emotional state even worse" and was "determined to exaggerate the fear of him abducting the children."

Sarah had wanted to submit reports to the court from her husband's GP, psychiatrist and police officers who had expressed concern about his violent behaviour. These, she was told, would be irrelevant.

The welfare officer acknowledged that Dave had been suicidal, but stated that "he now seemed better." "He was bamboozled by the fact that Dave was articulate and a doctor," says Sarah.

"Domestic violence cuts across all classes, but clever middle-class men have more allowances made for them."

On the day of the hearing, Sarah was persuaded to reach a "door of court" agreement. "I was adamant he should not have the children unsupervised, but, after about three hours of legal argument, I was beaten down. If I didn't agree, I was told I would have to go into the witness stand, we would end up carrying out character assassinations of each other, and then the judge would grant him weekend access anyway."

Hilary Saunders is a former policy adviser to Women's Aid and the author of the Twenty-Nine Child Homicides report. She says: "Countless abused women would tell you that what happened to Sarah at the door of court has also happened to them."

Domestic violence features in two-thirds of all child access cases, yet in less than one per cent of all cases is unsupervised contact denied. The problem, Saunders adds, is our "horrendously complex" legal system which makes the assumption that contact with a parent is in the best interests of the child, regardless of that child's safety.

Last year, in response to the Twenty-Nine Child Homicides report, the Family Justice Council issued new guidelines which state that safety must be paramount. It's a step forward, but, according to Saunders, "until that guidance is contained in legislation, there will always be problems."

For Sarah, anniversaries and birthdays have come and gone. Nina would be 18 now and Jack 17. "Christmas and birthdays are particularly harrowing, but ordinary days can also become hard work."

"Just two days ago, I woke up and had forgotten they were dead. Through the night they had been in my dreams and they had been alive.

120

It was lovely, but each time I wake up I have to go through that acute pain again, and I come down with a horrendous bump."

Mostly, her mind does not dwell any more on the day Nina and Jack were murdered. "But when I hear of another case I go straight back there and I feel sick."

She recalls the police coming to her door and, later, the sight of Jack and Nina through the glass wall of the mortuary, their faces still stained with traces of her lipstick that they had been playing with earlier that day.

She never saw Dave's body, "and afterwards I wished I had, because every so often I see someone who looks like him and I have that irrational thought: 'What if he's not really dead?'

In the immediate aftermath, she stayed with her parents. But when she could no longer endure the sight of other children going to school and normal life happening all around her, she went to Greece where she worked in a bar and learnt to pretend life was a gas.

"Every now and then I would fall apart, but mostly I held myself together in public. It became invaluable training for survival."

The following year, she embarked upon a relationship for which she wasn't emotionally ready. Out of it, however, came George, who has been her salvation and given her purpose. She loves him totally but is aware that she is an anxious mother.

"I try not to stifle him. I'll often phone a friend to ask, 'Am I being normal?'?

George has always known that he had a brother and sister who died, and when he was five, Sarah explained what happened to them. "I made a pact with myself that I would never lie to him."

She's had a couple of long-term relationships, but placing her complete trust in someone else is a lot to ask. "I'm happiest when I am self-reliant," she asserts.

She's also permanently restless. Her current home is the 14th in as many years. With each move she takes with her a collection of Nina and Jack's treasures and toys. Jack's teddy bear sits on her bed and in her perpetual ironing pile is a pair of Nina's navy-blue school tights that she can't bear to remove.

Her feelings towards her husband have been through a sea change over the years. "I don't forgive him, but I no longer hate him. I feel sorry for him, because he also became a victim. He needed help and in his own way he was crying out for it."

All of them, she says, were betrayed by a flawed legal system that enabled her husband to kill Nina and Jack by placing them in his care.

"That massive sense of betrayal will never go away, but I live in hope that there will be changes. Nina and Jack shouldn't be dead, and every time another child is allowed to die, it is an insult to their memory. It's saying, we don't care about learning lessons. As their mother, I cannot just stand by and let that happen."